Obie's Opus

Obie Yadgar

Stories, anecdotes and curiosities
Behind the classical music radio microphone

Bloomington, IN   authorHOUSE®   Milton Keynes, UK

AuthorHouse™
1663 Liberty Drive, Suite 200
Bloomington, IN 47403
www.authorhouse.com
Phone: 1-800-839-8640

AuthorHouse™ UK Ltd.
500 Avebury Boulevard
Central Milton Keynes, MK9 2BE
www.authorhouse.co.uk
Phone: 08001974150

First published by AuthorHouse   3/20/2007

ISBN: 978-1-4259-9344-3 (sc)

Library of Congress Control Number: 2007900633

Printed in the United States of America
Bloomington, Indiana

This book is printed on acid-free paper.

Table of Contents

Overture

I have listened to the radio all my life. When just a boy, with the lights off in the family room where the old Philips reigned, basking in the soft glow from the dial, I spent hours being transported by the radio to lands I would probably never see. Listening to the radio opened windows into languages and cultures I could only dream about. Outside our home, the real world went by. Inside, I scanned my world with one hand on the radio knob, a cup of tea on the table beside me.

In Vietnam, while I served as a U.S. Army combat correspondent, my little transistor radio helped me escape to corners far away from the war's cruelty and stupidity, ugliness and waste, death and destruction. Every day my little radio gave me one more chance to hear exotic music and voices just in case it would be my last.

An Assyrian growing up in Tehran, Iran, I discovered early on that our radio was my ticket to places I had only read about, or seen in Hollywood movies. I imagined *myself* as the fifth Musketeer, fighting for justice alongside D'Artagnan. I saw *me* falling in love with the portrait of Gene Tierney, the way Dana Andrews did, in the film classic *Laura*. And, of course, *I* was William Holden dancing by that river in Kansas with the stunning Kim Novak, in *Picnic*.

Like all of youth, mine had its own joys and sorrows, curiosities and anxieties, and my radio was the doorway that made my dreams more magical. I would turn the dial and find my own private box seat in the world's concert halls. The music was as diverse as the languages I heard, and as colorful. It opened my ears to sound. That same sound created in me a thirst for music as diverse as the lands that composed it. The languages I heard filled my ears with tones which years later I would use as a writer and classical music radio announcer: The stories in *Obie's Opus* are from those radio days.

I still listen to radio. Not as much as I did when I was a boy with a head full of dreams and all the time in the world to play with them. Radio has lost part of its luster in this age of explosive technology, where you can link up with any part of the world in an instant. But I still see it sparkle.

My old radio, the one from the old country, is gone along with many of the other things from my youth. My new radio is a big black box with enough buttons to decorate a troop of dragoons. It probably pulls in far more radio stations than I ever could in the old days. But it is not the same.

Some late nights now when I take a break from writing, I brew a pot of tea and sit in the dark pushing the buttons and spinning the dial on my new radio. From the study in my home in Milwaukee, Wisconsin, I once again travel to places beyond my reach. In those late hours, I dust off the gallery of images tucked away in my memory, taking flight once again to the far away places I visited as a child.

The only thing missing is the glow from the old Philips' dial.

Prelude

I can only describe this book as some of life's observations behind the radio microphone, as illustrated by stories, anecdotes and curiosities from the world of classical music. I have been a classical music radio announcer for much of my broadcast career. While also holding titles as program director and music director, they have meant little to me. What matters most is to slip behind the microphone and just do it: play glorious music and chat with the audience.

Since I have enjoyed a parallel career as a writer, therefore, I have always been the writer playing radio. Because of this, I am told I see things differently from many other announcers behind the radio microphone. For instance, a rainy day to me is an *introspective day*, or a *day to sit by the window and watch the world go by*, or a *day to stay home with a samovar of tea and a Russian novel*. A sunny day is a *perfect day to put on a pair of fancy shades and float around the city*. And so on. I create each show as if writing a new short story. The mood, the music and the conversation are elements of that story. That I pepper my conversations with stories, anecdotes and curiosities from the world of classical music, listeners tell me the practice adds to their appreciation of classical music.

These tidbits are also a way of casting the great composers, conductors and musicians into mortal roles. After all, Beethoven was also a human being, as were Mozart, Brahms and all the rest. They wrote magnificent music, yes, but they also woke up everyday and had breakfast. I can't remember how precisely I came across each anecdote. Some I have read, but most my listeners have recounted to me, as they often call on the studio phone off the air – I have always been a sucker for a good chat. How true these stories are is hard to tell, even though most have been around a long time. Where my listeners picked them up I have no idea. How the stories have changed with each telling I can only guess. For years listeners have asked me to publish them in a book. So OBIE'S OPUS. I dedicate this book to my listeners with all my love and respect, for you have taught me so much about classical music, and added so much to my love of radio. Thanks for putting up with me all these years, and may good fortune swim in your lane.

Obie Yadgar
Milwaukee, Wisconsin

Biography

As a boy growing up in Tehran, Obelit ("Obie") Yadgar, who is of
Assyrian heritage, spent hours listening to shortwave radio. Years later
in America, he drifted into radio as announcer, mostly for classical
music and jazz. He has had stints at KDIG, San Diego; WEKT,
upstate New York; and KWMU, St. Louis; WFMR, Milwaukee;
WUWM, Milwaukee; and WNIB, Chicago. Obie, who also has
enjoyed a career as writer, has written for magazines and newspapers,
with a tour of duty in Vietnam as a U.S. Army combat correspondent.
He has written video scripts, radio essays and short stories. Currently
Obie contributes essays to WBEZ, Chicago. "Will's Music," his first
novel, was published by AuthorHouse, in 2005, and is available from
authourhouse.com. Currently Obie is working on a second novel. He
has two daughters, Sonja and Sadie, and he currently lives with his
wife Judy in Milwaukee, Wisconsin.

Obie's Opus

*The most wasted day is that in
which we have not laughed*

$\mathcal{N}$icholas de Chamfort (1741-1794), the French writer and humorist, said that "The most wasted day is that in which we have not laughed." One of the biggest laughs I've had was the morning Charlie and Gilbert, neutered male pet cats at WNIB, Chicago, had a love fest in the studio during my live newscast. I could never tell that story on my program. The following stories I did tell many times on the air, confident they drew at least a smile from the audience every time.

♠ An aging actor called on Offenbach on the morning of October 5, 1880. "How is he?" he asked. "Mr. Offenbach is dead," said the servant. "He died peacefully, without knowing anything about it." The actor sighed. "Ah, he will be surprised when he finds out."

♠ Basso Andrew Foldi, who was doing *Die Fledermaus* with the San Francisco Opera, was stuck with a dressing room on the third floor. One day, when the stage manager called for places, the elevator was packed with equipment. Stepping back as the door closed, Foldi yelled, "They can schlep garbage or they can schlep Foldi, but garbage and Foldi they cannot schlep."

♠ In his first job as organist and choirmaster in Arnstadt, Bach was criticized for disregarding rules – organ introductions too long, hymns too short, harmonies too strange, and so on. People also couldn't understand why he had taken a certain young lady into the choir loft. She's my cousin, Bach explained, and I was showing her my organ.

3

♠ An organ grinder irritated Jacques Halevy by playing tunes from Rossini's opera *The Barber of Seville* outside his window. So Halevy told him, "I will pay you one Louis d'Or if you will stand outside Rossini's window and play one of my tunes." Replied the organ grinder: "But Rossini paid me two Louis d'Or to play his music outside your window."

♠ Leopold Stokowsky was the first to conduct an orchestra in the U.S. without a score or a baton. "Isn't it a shame that Stokowsky cannot read music?" a lady once said. "Imagine how wonderful he would be if he just knew how."

♠ Somebody told George Gershwin's father that Einstein's theory of relativity took 20 years to develop and yet it was only three pages long. "It must have been very close print," said papa Gershwin.

♠ Backstage, this lady tells the pianist she enjoyed his encore and wants her daughter to learn it. "Madam, that music was Robert Schumann's Opus 23 No. 4," says the pianist. "Oh, how wonderful," beams the lady, "because I just love opuses."

♠ Berlioz had a mistress named Marie, who was a dreadful singer. A neighbor woman once passed the house and heard screaming. Apparently Marie was practicing. The woman cringed and moved on. On the way home later that afternoon, when she heard the screaming again, the woman crossed herself and cried out, "My God, it's three o'clock and the baby still isn't born yet."

♠ During a bad rehearsal, a frustrated Toscanini announced to the musicians, "After I die, I shall return to earth as the doorkeeper of a bordello and I won't let any one of you in."

♠ While in London, Haydn was going to have a growth on his nose removed by his friend Dr. John Hunter. On the day of the surgery, an anxious Haydn found four big bruisers waiting to hold him down during the procedure. No way! Freaking out, Haydn marched out of the doctor's office – with the lump still riding on his beak.

♠ Jean Sibelius gave parties in Helsinki that lasted for days. During one party, conductor Bruno Walter had to leave for a guest conducting engagement in a nearby town. When he returned, the party was still going on. Just as Walter was pouring a glass of wine, Sibelius drifted over and, shaking a finger, announced, "Shame, Bruno, so long you were in the bathroom."

♠ Jean Le Franc, Boston Symphony's first violist, liked only classical music. Frank Sinatra was once introduced to him backstage. "Do you know Frank Sinatra?" he was asked. "I know Franck Sonata," said Le Franc, "but who is this?"

♠ Verdi's friend was shocked to find the composer's vacation home stuffed with organ barrels. Verdi explained that all the city organ players knew he was coming and were planning on cranking out tunes from his operas. The only way he could have a peaceful vacation, he said, was to rent all the barrel organs in town and park them in his house until the end of his vacation.

♠ Oscar Levant was kidding around when he told a Hollywood producer that a competitive studio was thinking of taking an option on Dvorak's *Symphony from the New World*. "Thanks for the tip," said the producer. "We'll outbid them."

♠ "Going on the railroad is for me like going to be hanged," said Johann Strauss Jr., who had train phobia. So when traveling by train, he would draw the blinds and spent a lot of time stretched out under the seat – with plenty of champagne.

♠ Brahms and a friend were discussing a singer who had a beautiful voice but was ugly. The friend held that artistry was more important than looks. "For a musician perhaps," said Brahms, "but I prefer looks."

♠ Deadlines didn't faze Rossini. "The best time to compose an overture is the evening before opening night," he once said. "Nothing primes inspiration more than necessity, whether it be the presence of a copyist waiting for your work or the prodding of an impresario tearing at his hair. In my time all the impresarios in Italy were bald at thirty."

♠ *I had miscued a CD and was playing a Chopin nocturne instead of the last movement of Beethoven's sonata known as the Tempest when a listener called the studio phone off the air and told me this one*: In the last movement of Beethoven's Ninth Symphony, where there's a long passage when the string basses don't play, the principal bass says to his section, "Let's go across the street and get a few beers." So they quietly shuffle off. Several beers later one player says it's time for them to get back. The principal bass says not to worry, because he's tied the conductor's score with strings and it'll take a while for him to untie it. So they have another round. Finally when they stumble back, the concertmaster looks at the assistant concertmaster and says, "You know, the conductor looks really worried." The assistant replies, "He has good reason. It's the bottom of the ninth, the score is tied, and the basses are loaded."

♠ Mischa Elman's father was also his agent, manager and accountant. One night, as Elman played the Chaconne by Bach, his father paced backstage clutching the little cashbox and glancing at his watch every few moments. Finally, running out of patience, he pointed to the cashbox and whispered, "Mischa, Mischa, can you hear me? Come on. Play a bit quicker. The bank is closing."

♠ Pianist Artur Rubinstein (1889-1982), who in the early years spoke no English, showed Rudolph Ganz in Chicago a letter he had received from a lady in Washington, D.C. "We are delighted that you will be giving your recital in Washington," read the letter. "Could you kindly include as an encore your celebrated piece, 'Kammenoi-Ostrow'?" Rubinstein, with help from Ganz, replied: "Dear Madame: Thank you for your kind letter. I would be delighted to play for you my celebrated 'Kammenois-Ostrow.' Unfortunately, it will not be possible. I am dead. Sincerely yours, A. Rubinstein." *The music was composed by the Russian Anton Rubinstein (1829-1894).*

♠ An angry Arturo Toscanini once chastised a musician for playing badly. After the musician shot back an insult, Toscanini ordered him off the stage. As he was leaving, the player turned to Toscanini and shouted, "Nuts to You." Toscanini fired back, "It's too late to apologize."

♠ Henryk Wieniawski played Reverie and Caprice at a concert honoring Berlioz. "Never have I heard an artist who has so completely caught my meaning and has so wonderfully interpreted it," declared Berlioz afterward. Backstage, Wieniawski said to Mendelssohn, "I am glad I got through it. I never had such a task in my life. I have not the remotest idea what I have been playing or what the piece can be about."

♠ Mozart was rehearsing *Don Giovanni* in Prague and the soprano couldn't get Zerlina right. This is when Don Giovanni makes advances at Zerlina. Mozart had to do something, so he sneaked backstage and at the right moment grabbed her by the waist. She shrieked. "You see, madam," said Mozart, "this is the way an innocent young woman screams when her virtue is in danger."

♠ Offenbach frequently forgot to button his trousers and his wife had to remind him of it. Finally they developed a code whereby she would start talking about *Monsieur Durant*, which was a signal to Offenbach to button his fly.

♠ Sir Arthur Sullivan found Rossini trying out a piece of music he had written and asked what it was. "It's my dog's birthday," said Rossini, "and I write a little piece for him every day."

♠ On the coach to Florence with three Jesuits and a surly Venetian woman, Mendelssohn wrote to a friend that the driver was rude and obnoxious. "He doesn't allow you to stop and lets you starve and thirst," he said. Invariably driving through suppertime, the coachman would stop at an inn after midnight, when all the rooms were already booked, to be back on the road again at 3 a.m. "At midday he stops for five hours, choosing without fail an inn where there's nothing to eat," wrote Mendelssohn. "He drives his six German miles a day *piano* while the sun shines *fortissimo*." In the end, about half day's journey from Florence, Mendelssohn found another mode of transportation, not before giving the driver a piece of his mind. "I told him to drive to the devil – advice he didn't appreciate," wrote Mendelssohn.

♠ A Hollywood producer was ecstatic to hear he could get Maurice Ravel to do the music for his movie. Except that he was mistaking *Ravel*, the Impressionist composer of Bolero, for half of the popular songwriting team of Gordon and *Revel*.

♠ Mozart, a practical joker, had written a piece that his good friend Haydn was unable to play no matter how hard he tried. The culprit was a note in the center of the keyboard, when the right hand played in high treble and the left in low bass. "I have only two hands," complained Haydn. "Nobody can play that with two hands." Mozart said that he could, and proceeded to play from the start. When he reached the part in question, he bent over and struck the note with his nose. "Well," said Haydn. "With a nose like yours, it becomes easier."

♠ In 1928, an elderly lady in New York told Jascha Heifetz, "Your violin sounded wonderful this evening." Heifetz put the violin to his ear and said, "I don't hear anything."

♠ Liszt played up to his audience like today's rock stars, orchestrating the movements of his flowing hair and the quivering of his lips and nostrils to stress emotion. When playing sensuous music, he fixed his eyes on a beautiful woman in the audience. He also arranged for women to faint during his concerts. One woman once missed her cue, upsetting Liszt so much that he fainted.

♠ Richard Strauss was conducting his tone poem *Don Juan* and the string players were not delivering what he wanted. So just before the rising phrase at the opening of *Don Juan*, he yelled, "Gentlemen, I would ask those of you who are married to play this phrase as though you were engaged."

♠ Rudolf Serkin made his piano concert debut in Berlin with the Busch Chamber Players, performing Bach's Fifth Brandenburg Concerto. When the audience called for an encore from Serkin, the young pianist asked Adolph Busch what he should play. "Why, the Goldberg Variations," joked Busch, pushing him out onto the stage. Serkin did so, with all the repeats. An hour later, only three other people were left in the concert hall: Busch, pianist Artur Schnabel, and the critic Alfred Einstein, all of whom applauded warmly.

♠ Strolling with a friend in New York City, Fritz Kreisler came to a fish store. He stopped suddenly and threw a salute at the rows of lifeless fish with their glossy eyes and opens mouths. "That reminds me," he declared. "I have a concert tonight."

♠ Mozart's mind never stopped working. This especially frustrated his barber, because Mozart would not sit long enough for the man to do his job and that he would have to chase after him with comb and ribbon.

♠ Pianist Artur Schnabel and conductor Otto Klemperer were rehearsing a Beethoven concerto when they disagreed on the tempo in a certain passage. One wanted it faster while the other slower. "Herr Schnabel, the conductor is here," said Klemperer. Schnabel shot back, "Ah, Klemperer is there and I am here, but where is Beethoven?"

♠ Vladimir de Pachmann, at a recital in 1920, found the piano bench too low, so he left the stage and returned with a phone book. It was still not quite the right height. So he tore a page from the book and sat down again. Now everything was right. *Comedian Victor Borge used to kill the audience with this routine.*

♠ Toward the end of his life and almost completely deaf, Beethoven resorted to using his notebook to communicate. Needing a tailor once, here is a conversation he held with a friend:

Beethoven: Can you recommend me a tailor? Mine is a fool. This frock coat fits me like a sack. I look as if I had stolen it.

Friend: I will send you to the tailor who works for me.

Beethoven: Does he call himself an artist in clothes?

Friend: No. He remains true to the honest old German name for his craft.

Beethoven: My stupid tailor cannot even sew on buttons properly. I have worn this jacket barely half a year, and five buttons are already absent without leave.

♠ Mendelssohn's manuscripts were confiscated in Venice by customs authorities thinking they contained secret codes. It took quite a bit of talking by Mendelssohn to convince them otherwise.

♠ Kreisler and Rachmaninoff were playing Grieg's Second Violin Sonata when Kreisler got lost in the score. He turned to Rachmaninoff and whispered, "Where are we?" Rachmaninoff answered, "Carnegie Hall."

♠ A lady admirer once complained that the coda of an Edvard Grieg composition lacked the sparkle of the rest of it. "Ah, yes," Grieg shrugged. "At that point inspiration gave out and I had to finish without it."

♠ Heifetz was having dinner with Mischa Elman when a bellboy brought an envelop to the table inscribed "To the greatest violinist in the world." Heifetz passed it over and said, "You open it, Mischa." Elman protested, "Oh, no, you open it, Jascha." Well they both opened it. The message inside read: "Dear Fritz . . ." *The letter was addressed to Fritz Kreisler, another famous violinist.*

♠ Beethoven had not been to Swan Tavern in Vienna for days. When he finally came in, Ludwig Spohr asked him, "What has happened to you, master? I hope you haven't been ill." Beethoven growled, "I haven't, but my boots have, and as I own only one pair, I was under house arrest."

♠ During rehearsals, Richard Strauss told a player, "No, no, that's a half-note. It isn't dotted." The player studied the score, confused. "Excuse me, maestro," he said. "There's a fly speck there. I thought it was a dot." Strauss gave the cue to start, only to stop abruptly and think. "No," he said, "the fly was right."

♠ Otto Klemperer was conducting a modern piece when a player, fed up with the music, stomped out. Watching him, Klemperer remarked, "Thanks God somebody understands."

♠ Hans Von Bulow, getting a resounding ovation at his recital, played several encores and people kept on applauding. Eventually, anxious to get off the stage, he motioned for silence. "If you don't stop this applause," he announced, "I will play all of Bach's 48 preludes and fugues, from beginning to end." And that sent everybody home.

♠ Leopold Stokowsky was conducting Beethoven's Leonora Overture. The two climaxes of the piece are each followed by a trumpet passage that is played off stage. In this performance, the climax came and Stokowsky heard nothing off stage. The second climax came and still nothing off stage. After the overture, Stokowsky stormed backstage only to find the trumpet player arguing with the stagehand and the stagehand telling him, "I tell you, you can't play that thing back here. There's a concert going on."

♠ Enrico Caruso was a notorious prankster. In Act I of Puccini's *La Boheme*, Rodolfo, pretending to search for Mimi's lost key, gropes in the dark and touches Mimi's little cold hand. He sings "*Che gelida manina*" (How cold your hand is). One time when he sang the part, Caruso dug up a hot potato from his pocket and pressed it into Mimi's cold hand – "*Se la lasci riscaldar*" (Let me warm it here in mine). Another time, in the midst of a soprano aria, Caruso peered at the singer's wide-open mouth and whispered, "How would you like a nice, juicy steak?"

♠ Stokowsky enjoyed taking the orchestra by surprise during rehearsals. On such occasions he would sweep in, mount the podium, and announce something like, "Strauss, Letter F," and instantly begin conducting. This usually caught his players unprepared. One time when only a few players managed to find their place in the score, Stokowsky barked, "Too late." A player, unruffled, stood up and announced, "Too soon." Stokowsky smiled and proceeded with rehearsals

♠ Rossini didn't like composing overtures. He said, "I never composed any overture to my opera *Moses*, which is the easiest way of all."

Some days it doesn't pay to get out of bed

There were days in radio when nothing seemed to go right, starting with battling potholes in Chicago roads and ending with two recordings skipping in a row. Those are the days you want to stay in bed. George Bizet, the composer of *Carmen*, had the perfect answer for the frustrations of his life: "In order to succeed today we must be either dead or German." But that was not the end of it for old George:

♠ Bizet had an unlucky streak running through him. For instance: (1) He would kill himself trying to meet a deadline only to find out the production was delayed. (2) Soon after finishing his symphony he misplaced the manuscript, only to be discovered years after his death. (3) He wrote a bad review of a concert and the conductor challenged him to a duel. (4) He entered a two-man composing contest and came in second. (5) The *pieces de resistance* was the time when he tapped on his sweetheart's window just at the moment her mother was emptying a chamber pot from the window directly above him. *S-P-L-A-S-H!*

♠ Borodin was a composer as well as a scientist, a doctor, and general in the Russian army. He was also forgetful. One morning he thought he left his house in full uniform, medals and all, only to realize that he had forgotten his pants.

♠ Strauss wrote the music for the operetta *Eine Nacht in Venedig* (A Night in Venice) without fully knowing the plot. So it bombed.

♠ In his youth, Wagner wrote a play with such a complicated plot that by the end of the second act some 40 characters had been killed. Since he still had a play to finish, he brought back some of the key people as ghosts.

*When a guy gets stabbed in the back
and instead of bleeding, he sings*

Or Some Of Life's Ironies

$\mathcal{E}$d Gardner's complete quote reads: "Opera is when a guy gets stabbed in the back and instead of bleeding, he sings." I find that comment not only funny, but also ironic. Then again, the musical world is full of irony.

♠ Offenbach gave his valet a good reference even though he fired him. Why did you fire the guy if he was that good? a friend wondered. Offenbach explained that although the man was a good valet, he was bad for a composer to have around. "He always beat my clothes outside my door and the tempo was invariably wrong," he added.

♠ "Yankee Doodle," dating back to the French and Indian Wars, was derived from a song British regulars sang poking fun at the uniformed colonial soldiers fighting alongside them. Later, as they fought the British, the Colonials remembered the sting and took "Yankee Doodle" as a battle song.

♠ Pushkin was killed in a duel in 1837. Yet his killer, the French officer Georges d'Anthes, lived for another 58 years.

♠ Pasadoble is a one-step dance literally called a double step.

♠ On March 14, 1947, a concert guide magazine ran the following item: "Descendants of Franz Schubert live in misery." On the occasion of 150th anniversary of Schubert's birth, the Vienna Philharmonic Orchestra gave them a life pension. *Go figure – because Schubert was never married to have descendants.*

♠ Arnold Schoenberg was once turned down for a Guggenheim Fellowship.

♠ Berlioz arranged orchestral pieces from his failed opera *Benvenuto Cellini* into a composition titled Concert Overture for Benvenuto Cellini. The audience hated it. Gambling on human nature, he changed the title to Roman Carnival Overture – a whopping hit.

♠ Schubert got the idea for writing the quartet *Death and the Maiden* while grinding his coffee.

♠ In 1851 in Hamburg, the young Brahms left a package of songs and piano pieces at Robert and Clara Schumann's hotel for them to look at. But they had no time for him and the package was returned unopened. Years later they would become his friends and champion his music.

♠ Robert Schumann first saw Clara Wieck when she was 9 years old and he in his late teens. She played piano with a trio. This was about the time Schumann began studying with her father Friedrich Wieck. Clara impressed Schumann as a prodigy, but he thought she wasn't much to look at. Years later Robert and Clara Schumann's became a great romantic story.

♠ Rossini's final great composition was the *Little Solemn Mass*. He left directions that it had to be sung by 12 singers of three sexes. The *Mass* was also accompanied by his open letter: "Dear God, here it is, my poor little *Mass*, done with a little skill, a bit of heart, and that's about all. Be Thou Blessed, and admit me to Paradise."

♠ Sibelius rarely invited musicians to his home. "They talk of nothing but money and jobs," he complained. "Give me a businessman every time. They really are interested in music and art."

♠ The manuscript of Schubert's opera *Claudine Von Villa Bella* had been in position of Schubert's good friend Anselm Huttenbrenner, whose servants had used pages from it to light the fire.

♠ Herbert Von Karajan was Berlin Philharmonic's conductor for 30 years. He also guest conducted the Vienna Philharmonic, among many other orchestras. He once told a journalist: "If I tell the Berliners to step forward, they do it. If I tell the Viennese to step forward, they do it, but then they ask why."

♠After Chopin's death, his sister Ludwika took with her some 200 letters from George Sand to Chopin. Fearing Russian border guards, she left the letters in care of a friend of Chopin's. In 1851, the letters were discovered and copied by Alexandre Dumas. The originals were sent back to George Sand, who burned them. The copies were lost.

♠ Richard Strauss conducted well into old age. Once after conducting *Der Rosenkavalier*, he whispered to the concertmaster, "This is awfully long, isn't it?" The concertmaster replied, "You composed it, maestro." Strauss declared, "Yes, but I didn't think I would have to conduct it."

♠ In 1928 in Paris, George Gershwin asked Igor Stravinsky how much he would charge to give him lessons in orchestration. "How much do you make a year?" asked Stravinsky. "A hundred thousand dollars," Gershwin said. Stravinsky thought a moment and said, "How about your giving me lessons?"

♠ For a man who wrote so much dance music, Johann Strauss Jr. couldn't dance.

♠ Brahms autographed Frau Strauss' fan with the opening measures of "The Blue Danube Waltz" and signed it *"Alas, not by Johannes Brahms."*

♠ Heinrich Schutz (1585-1672), who was chapel master for the Elector of Saxony, had a magnificent bass in the choir. Not only unreliable, the man also drank a keg of wine a day. Schutz defended him by explaining that he had an exceptionally wide throat that needed more moistening than ordinary ones. *You tell 'em, man.*

♠ Vivaldi was unsuited for the priesthood, although the priesthood was one way the poor could receive an education. Also, according to a story, on the day Vivaldi was born – March 4, 1678 – an earthquake struck Venice. His mother vowed that if they survived, her son would become a priest – and so Vivaldi had to fulfill her wish.

♠ Franz Liszt, a Hungarian whose music is spiked with Hungarian nationalism, spoke no Hungarian.

♠ Beethoven was born at 934 Rheingasse Street in Bonn, Germany. That address is now No. 7 Rheingasse Street. The same street produced a number of other musical luminaries: Nicholas Simrock (who published Bach, Beethoven, Brahms and Dvorak); Ferdinand Ries (composer and Beethoven's friend); and Johann Peter Solomon (music impresario, responsible for Haydn's two trips to England).

♠ After Mozart's death in 1791, his wife Constanza moved to Copenhagen and married Georg Nissen. They had a good life together. When Nissen died, Constanza had his tombstone inscribed thusly: "Here rests Mozart's widow's second spouse."

♠ Years after Mozart's death, Beethoven's nephew said that Mozart's fingers were so bent from so many performances that he could not cut his steak. Constanza's second husband, Georg Nissen, corroborated that. He also said that aside from clavier playing, Mozart was clumsy in the use of his hands, and that Constanza had to cut his steak as though he were a child. They both said that one reason Mozart wanted a life as a composer rather than a performer was that he knew he had only a few years of playing left because of the condition of his hands – he had suffered from arthritis since his youth.

♠ The Met, fearing the audience would not understand *Schwanda the Bagpiper*, by the Czech composer Jaromir Weinberger in the original Czech, translated it into German. *Go figure.*

♠ "Dixie," the Civil War era song, was written for a minstrel show by Dan Emmett, who was a Northerner. Horrified that the South used it, Emmett wrote new lyrics for the song, denouncing the Confederacy. It didn't work, and "Dixie" remained popular in the South.

♠ George Gershwin was always asking renowned composers for music lessons. He asked Arnold Schoenberg to take him on as a pupil, but Schoenberg refused, saying, "I would only make you a bad Schoenberg, and you're such a good Gershwin already."

♠ In 1712, Handel took a leave of absence from the court in Hanover and traveled to England to work for Queen Anne. By 1715, the Elector of Hanover, Handel's boss, was wondering where his composer was. Then the elector was brought to England to reign as George I, and things got embarrassing and difficult for Handel.

♠ Tchaikovsky made several attempts at writing an opera before he finished his first and saw it produced. *The Oprichnik* is about the secret police during the reign of Ivan the Terrible. The opera was popular until people lost their appetite for stories about the secret police.

♠ While saying mass, Vivaldi, who was an ordained priest, would often get musical ideas and have to dash away from the alter to jot them down. Finally he was brought before an inquisition, where blame was put on his musical genius. Although he escaped punishment, he was forbidden to say Mass again.

♠ In 1814, Roncole, Italy, was sacked and many people were killed, including women and children trying to hide in the town's church. The story goes that one mother survived with her child by hiding in the bell tower. That child was Giuseppe Verdi.

♠ Wagner's biggest admirer was the conductor Hans von Bulow, who also must have been the world's most broad-minded person. While Bulow was rehearsing Wagner's *Tristan und Isolde*, Wagner was having an affair with Bulow's wife Cosima. They had a baby girl. Rather than being outraged, Bulow went so far as naming the baby Isolde.

♠ "The Battle Hymn of the Republic," set to Julia Howe's flaming poetry, was popular with firemen and negro slave church congregations long before the North turned it into a martial song during the Civil War.

♠ In 1790, when Haydn left on his first trip to London, Mozart had tears in his eyes. "I fear, my father, that this is the last time we shall see each other," he said. When Mozart died in 1791, Haydn was still in London.

♠ Schubert was one of the torchbearers at Beethoven's funeral in Vienna. Later that day, he and friends got together at the tavern Zum Schloss Eisenstadt, and drank to Beethoven. Schubert then proposed a toast: "To the one we have just buried" – he hesitated a moment – "and to the one who is next." Two years later he himself was dead.

♠ Countess Marie d'Agoult, Liszt's lover, said that when she first met Liszt at a party at Chopin's apartment in Paris, she thought he was the most extraordinary man she had ever known. She saw a tall and slender figure with a pallid face. His eyes were sea green that flashed like fire, she said. Years earlier, an acquaintance of Liszt's had described his smile as "like the glitter of a dagger in sunlight."

♠ Some guy, who had nothing better to do, took it upon himself to find out just how blue the Danube River was. He concluded that on 255 days the river was green; on 60 days it was gray; on 40 days it was yellow; and on 10 days it was brown. That's 365 days when the Danube was anything but blue.

♠ Brahms told his father that if he ever needed comfort, something to lift his spirit, he should read their score of Handel's oratorio *Saul*. "I'm sure you'll find there whatever you need," said the young Brahms. Years later, when the elder Brahms was in financial trouble, he took his son's advice and opened the score, only to find money tucked onto each page.

♠ It is said that Beethoven was a dreadful dancer; the guy just couldn't move to the beat.

♠ Because of Leopold Mozart's rebellious nature, his mother ignored him, as she did his children Wolfgang and Nannerl.

♠ Rossini was composing a duet in bed when the page fell onto the floor. Rather than get out of bed, he wrote a whole new duet. Later a friend stopped by and picked up the sheet, so Rossini added another part to the duet and made it a trio.

♠ "If we could awaken a mummified pharaoh of the 13th century B.C. in a modern concert hall, he would recognize practically nothing but the sound of the harp parts" – Cecil Forsyth.

♠ In 1792, the mayor of Strasbourg asked Rouget de Lisle, a captain in the French garrison, to write a marching song. Rouget de Lisle composed the "Battle Song of the Army of the Rhine." Four months later, on August 10, when soldiers from Marseilles marched on the Tuilleries, they sang that song – which became famous as "La Marseillaise." Rouget de Lisle, far from a revolutionary, was a loyalist.

♠ Pierre Monteaux signed a 25-year contract as principal conductor of the London Symphony on the condition that he could have an option for another 25 years. Monteaux was 80 years old. *Cheers!*

♠ Prior to 1939, hardly anyone knew of Antonio Vivaldi. Scholars knew of him from about 20 transcriptions Bach had made of his works. In September 1939, the city of Sienna, Italy, held a six-day music festival in which Vivaldi was performed – and people liked what they heard.

♠ Toscanini revered Verdi so much that he once agreed to conduct a Verdi festival on the condition that it would be gratis. Another conductor, jealous of Toscanini but unaware of the arrangement, demanded he be paid one lira more than whatever Toscanini received. The management gladly accepted – and wrote him a check for one lira.

♠ Mozart's sister Marianne, called Nannerl, was a few years older than him, but she lived to be 78. Mozart died at 35.

♠ Beethoven studied piano, violin and viola, mostly at home under his father. But often the young Ludwig ignored the printed score and played things from his head, frustrating his father. Later when his father seriously listened to his son play, he told him, "Don't you ever stop doing that in spite of what I have told you."

♠ In 1848, Johann Strauss Sr. wrote the Radetzky March in honor of Field Marshall Count Josef Radetzky, whose Austrian army had defeated the Italians over the Kingdom of Sardinia. Later, when Radetzky was forced to put down an Austrian uprising, Strauss was made a scapegoat for writing the march that honored Radetzky. In the short time he had left to live, his reputation did not recover.

♠ On Christmas Day, 1790, on his way to London, Haydn stopped in Bonn, where he dined with the Elector of Bonn, and where the court orchestra and chorus performed one of his masses. The orchestra included a 20-year-old genius named Ludwig Van Beethoven.

♠ Opera didn't make its way into Russia until the 17th century. Czar Alexis imported a German company to mount an opera titled *The Acts of Artaxerxes*. The production was part of a birthday celebration for the new Czarevich, who grew up to be Peter the Great. The Czar even built a theatre for the occasion at his summer palace at Preobrazhenskoye. Yet Peter the Great developed little interest in music.

♠ Offenbach's concertmaster at the 1876 World Fair in Philadelphia was a young Washingtonian name John Philip Sousa.

♠ The Austrian Empress Maria Theresa found the way Mozart and his father went about looking for employment for the young Wolfgang in European courts distasteful. She said they went "about the world like beggars." In 1771, she wrote to her son, Archduke Ferdinand, in Milan, and advised him to ignore the Mozarts. "Do not burden yourself with such useless people," she said. In subsequent years the only things Mozart got from the Viennese court were commissions for musical scraps.

♠ In 1905, librettists Victor Leon and Leo Stein offered Richard Heuberger material for an operetta based on the French farce *L'Attache*, but he failed to come up with music for it. They then turned to Franz Lehar, a Hungarian composer working in Vienna. Right up to the premiere the operetta was still untitled. The title of *The Merry Widow* was the result of a mistake. Some high official, trying to get free tickets for the show from the management, referred to the operetta as *Die Lastige Witwe* (The Annoying Widow). Franz Lehar thought he heard *Die Lustige Witwe* (The Merry Widow), and thus the title.

♠ In 1787, with *Don Giovanni* a smash in Prague, Emperor Josef II appointed Mozart Imperial and Royal Chamber Composer in Vienna. The appointment was only to compose dance music. Mozart said the money he received was "too much for services I give and too little for what I am capable of giving." He wrote around 100 dances.

♠ Of the 600 works Mozart wrote only 70 were published in his lifetime.

♠ Francois Auber, the composer of such operas as *Fra Diavolo* and *Le Domino noir*, was born in a moving stagecoach. Except for a short stint as a clerk and songwriter in London, he rarely traveled outside Paris. Rather, he did the next best thing and packed his apartment with travel pictures.

♠ The first time Haydn met Empress Maria Theresa was when she had him thrashed for playing on the scaffolding at *Schoenbrunn*, her magnificent palace in Vienna. The next time he saw the queen was in 1773, on her visit to Esterhaza, the estate in the principality of Eisenstadt near Vienna, where Haydn was music director. He reminded her of the *Schoenbrunn* incident. Maria Theresa, by now a big fan of the great Haydn, declared, "That thrashing bore good fruit." Haydn named his Symphony No. 48 *Maria Theresa*.

♠ Toscanini was berating a radio broadcast performance of Beethoven's Seventh Symphony for poor phrasing, clumsy interpretation and lousy playing. When the recording was over, he launched into a diatribe about how the whole thing had missed the mark. It was his recording of the Beethoven's Seventh.

♠ Chopin met Clara Wieck in Leipzig, Germany, when she was 15. Later, when she became a famous pianist, Chopin said she was the only one in Germany who could play his music well.

♠ In 1791, when Mozart's *The Magic Flute* opened in Vienna, the playbill announced it as an "opera in two acts by Emanuel Schikaneder" – he was the producer. Only the small print at the bottom mentioned that it was composed by Mozart.

♠ Mendelssohn was a champion of young talent. When heading the Leipzig Conservatory of Music, he offered scholarships to students and provided free private lessons for the poor students. One such student, a 12-year-old Hungarian prodigy, grew up to be one of the greatest violinists in history – Joseph Joachim.

♠ Mstislav Rostropovich owned a Stradivari cello with a scratch caused by Napoleon Bonaparte's spur. A previous owner of the instrument had played it to an audience that included

Napoleon. Trying out the cello after the concert, Napoleon scratched it with his spur as he sat down. The scratch was never repaired.

♠ "Music and lyrics, no matter how good, can never pull a show through by themselves," said George Gershwin. "What moves a show along is two-four rhythm. You could say that a show travels on its two-fours, the way an army travels on its stomach."

♠ "She plays not a single bar without feeling. Even in the symphonies, she plays everything with expression, and no one could play an adagio with greater sensitivity than she. On the whole, I find that a woman who has talent plays more expressively than a man"—Leopold Mozart on the blind Italian violinist Regina Strinasacchi.

♠ Daniel Auber, who composed 45 operas, did not see a single performance of any of them. "If I knew I had to be present," he said, "I wouldn't be able to write a solitary note."

♠ Luigi Lablache (1794-1858) sang at three famous funerals: Haydn's, 1809, as boy soprano; Beethoven's, 1827, as bass; and Chopin's, 1849, as bass. At all three funerals he sang Mozart's *Requiem*.

♠ Bach's contemporaries considered him an old hat. After his death, a bundle of his manuscripts sold for the equivalent of $40. Some went for the equivalent of 10 cents apiece. Original manuscripts were used in butcher shops as wrapping paper.

♠ In 1830, when Chopin left Warsaw for Paris, he stopped in Wroclaw to visit the court music director Josef Ignaz Schnabel. Chopin was invited to try out the piano being used for rehearsals. He not only dazzled everyone, but his playing also scared the amateur pianist who was scheduled to play the concert so much that the poor guy canceled. Chopin ended up playing that concert.

Beechamisms

The renowned British conductor Sir Thomas Beecham (1879-1961) was also known for his urbane wit and acerbic charm. Stories about him abound, and I find them irresistible. These stories and anecdotes, known as *Beechamisms*, were a sure bet every time I used them on my radio programs. That's why I have built a special podium in OBIE'S OPUS for the unforgettable humor of the great Sir Thomas:

♠ While rehearsing Wagner's *Die Meistersinger*, Sir Thomas became irritated with the tenor. "Have you ever made love?" he asked him. "Yes, Sir Thomas," replied the tenor. "Do you consider yours a suitable way of making love to Eva?" inquired Sir Thomas. "Well, there are different ways of making love," offered the tenor. "Observing your grave, deliberate way of making music," declared Sir Thomas, "I was reminded of that estimable quadruped – the hedgehog."

♠ In 1914, in an address to the Manchester Royal College of Music, Sir Thomas said, "English singers cannot sing. There is only one I know who can walk on the stage with any grace. The others come on like a duck in a thunderstorm."

♠ Growing frustrated with a female cellist's performance during rehearsals, Sir Thomas finally told her: "You have between your legs the most sensitive instrument known to man, and all you can do is sit there and scratch it."

♠ "Good music is that which enters the ear with ease and leaves the mind with difficulty," said Sir Thomas. "Bad music is that which enters the ear with difficulty and leaves the mind with ease."

♠ "The English may not like music," confessed Sir Thomas, "but they absolutely love the noise it makes."

♠ Sir Thomas was the son of the famous manufacturer of Beecham's Pills. When he conducted the New York Philharmonic, people wondered whether the orchestra shouldn't change its name to the *New York Pillharmonic.*

♠ During a season in London of Russian operas, Sir Thomas was asked for his appraisal of the program. "It was a great success," he replied. "Nobody understood a word."

♠ While discussing modern composers, Sir Thomas was asked if he had heard of Stockhausen. "No," he replied, "but I believe I have trodden in some."

♠ The trombonist was frustrating him, so Sir Thomas said, "Are you producing as much sound as possible from that quaint and antique drainage system which you are applying to your face?" The message must have got through, because the trombonist proceeded to produce a big sound.

♠ Considering the almost interminable length of Wagner's operas, Sir Thomas was rehearsing *Gotterdammerung* when he said, "We've been rehearsing for two hours, and we're still playing the same old bloody tune."

♠ After several bows, Sir Thomas, growing tired, held up a hand and announced, "Ladies and gentlemen, when I was a very young conductor, I heard a deaf vicar in the front row say to his neighbor, 'Why is he bowing? The musicians did all the work.'" Pointing to the orchestra, Sir Thomas added, "So I shall leave, and you may applaud these gentlemen to your heart's content."

♠ Sir Thomas was running late for his concert at London's Covent Garden. His stand-in was ready to take over the pit when Sir Thomas threw his coat and hat aside and flew to the podium. The audience gave him a rousing welcome, and he took his bows. Raising his baton, then, Sir Thomas turned to the concertmaster and asked, "By the way, what opera are we doing tonight?" The concertmaster replied, "It's *La Boheme*, Sir Thomas." Said Sir Thomas, "Ah, to be sure," and gave the downbeat.

♠ During a production of Verdi's opera *Aida*, a horse on the stage suddenly began leaving its signature. Cool and calm, Sir Thomas said to the orchestra in a hushed voice, "Upon my word, gentlemen, he's a critic."

♠ While rehearsing, Sir Thomas heard too many wrong notes from a musician, so he stopped the orchestra. "We do not expect you to follow us all the time," he said to the musician, "but if you would have the goodness to keep in touch with us occasionally."

♠ Conducting Handel's *Messiah*, Sir Thomas announced to the chorus, "When we sing 'All we, like sheep, have gone astray,' might we please have a little more regret and a little less satisfaction?" One of the sopranos, a bit upset, said, "Sir Thomas, I'll have you know that I am a lady." Sir Thomas smiled and replied, "Madam, your secret is safe with me."

♠ Sir Thomas on the topic of women in the orchestra: "A pretty one will distract the other musicians, and an ugly one will distract me."

♠ Sir Thomas describing the harpsichord: "Sounds like two skeletons copulating on a corrugated tin roof."

♠ "Music is something that people can get on without," said Sir Thomas, "and if it costs too much, they will."

♠ "No opera star has yet died soon enough for me."

Only a lunatic would dance when sober

*L*ucius Annaeus Seneca (c 4 BC – AD 65), the Roman statesman, philosopher and writer, said: "Only a lunatic would dance when sober." I wonder what old Seneca would have said had he seen the fascinating historical and social course of dance?

♠ The minuet was introduced to the French court around 1652 during the reign of Louis XIV and soon overshadowed all other dances. Minuet is derived from the French *menu*, meaning "slender" or "small." It originated in Poitou. According to dance master Pierre Rameau – he flourished around 1725 – Beauchamp, Lully's ballet master in the court of Louis XIV, transformed the minuet into a court dance. In 1725, the minuet became a fashion in Europe.

♠ Jean-Baptiste Lully was the first composer to use ballerinas in his opera ballets.

♠ In 1681, the first professional female dancer appeared at the Paris Opera.

♠ Johann Strauss said the waltz "made some sorrows vanish" and it "gave back the joys of life."

♠ The waltz, regarded as the greatest dance craze of all time, began as a German dance popular with the lower classes in the dance halls and the beer gardens. In 1773, the waltz became fashionable in Vienna, and by 1792, in Berlin. "Waltzes and nothing but waltzes" was a popular expression. Since couples waltzing held each other close and whirled about passionately, the conservatives feared the dance would lead to moral decline. In time, as Beethoven and Schubert used it in their compositions, the waltz gained respect. Lanner and

Strauss helped it along even more. So did the Spanish composer Martin Y Soler, who included a waltz in his opera *Una Cosa Rora*. Eventually couples milked the passionate side of the waltz by floating to the dark side of the dance floor for a little smooching. Because of that, waltzing was banned in parts of Swabia and Switzerland. *Some of today's dances would definitely set knickers on fire.*

♠ The waltz was the earliest piece of music written for a first lady of the United States. She was Dolly Madison, who had encountered the dance in Europe. The dance tune was titled "Mrs. Madison's Waltz." *No idea who composed it.*

♠ The oldest known waltz tune is from 1770, the year Beethoven was born. It is a little gem called "Ach du lieber Augustin." *No idea who wrote that either.*

♠ Weber's "Invitation to the Dance" established the concert waltz.

♠ Bolero was invented in 1780 by the Spanish dancer Sebastiano Carezo.

♠ Jota is a lively dance invented in the 12th century by a Moor named Aben Tot.

♠ Bulerias, one of the most popular and exciting Flamenco dance forms, was developed in the 19th century by a Spanish singer named Loco Mateo (Mad Mathew).

♠ Gallito (Little Rooster), a pasadoble by Santiago Lope, was named after the bullfighter Gallito (Jose Gomez, 1895-1920), who was gored to death in the ring.

♠ Folia – of Spanish and Portuguese origin – was forbidden in Spain in the 16th century because of its sexual connotation. Men who were caught dancing it were sentenced to the galley boats for life and women banished to distant lands.

♠ Saraband, although initially risqué, was a stately dance invented in the 16th century by a Spanish musician named Zarabande, who might have taken it from a Persian dance called *Ser-band*.

Standing tall

*M*ore than anyone, Beethoven helped me to believe in myself, to be confident in what I did. Beethoven not only composed magnificent music, but he also possessed incredible strength and a profound sense of individuality. Beethoven was so sure of his powers, of himself, and so proud, that he once announced with defiance, "With whom need I be afraid of measuring my strength?" Beethoven stood tall.

♠ Ludwig Van Beethoven and his brother Johann, a businessman, did not get along. One New Year's Day, when Johann had bought a piece of land, he sent Ludwig a card and signed it: *"Johann Van Beethoven, landowner."* Ludwig crossed off his brother's name and returned the card, signed: *"Ludwig Van Beethoven, brain owner."*

♠ Alexander Pushkin, the Russian poet, was ordered by the secret police to rewrite *Boris Gudonov* for its subversive tone. Pushkin refused. Later *Boris Gudonov* became a famous opera by Modest Moussorgsky.

♠ In 1989, the Chicago Tribune ran a story about a young woman named Sonia Sudak who, while strolling in New York's Central Park and listening on her headphones to Vivaldi, was confronted by two teenage thugs demanding her radio. "Oh, you wouldn't want it," Sudak declared. "It only plays classical music." The thugs saw it as a no-win situation and slinked away.

♠ "True, my songs are sung at street corners, but only at the corners of the very best streets" – Oscar Straus.

♠ Pianist Vladimir de Pachmann, after being booed at a concert in Budapest, had the doors locked. He then pulled out an automatic pistol and put it next to him on the piano bench. Not a peep after that from the audience.

♠ Vivaldi was such a fast composer that he boasted he could compose all the parts of a concerto faster than a copyist could write them down.

♠ Franz Schubert auditioned for the director of the Vienna Choir Boys. Impressed with Schubert's singing, the director wondered how it was that he had never heard the songs before. "Of course," said Schubert. "It's because I wrote them."

♠ While court composer at Cothen, Bach was once passing through Dresden and was challenged by a promoter to a clavier duel with the French organist and composer Louis Marchand. Since Marchand was aware of Bach's prowess as organist and keyboard player and knew Bach would blow him away, he packed his bag and split town.

♠ Abbe Joseph Gelinek, a popular pianist in Vienna, boasted that he would show the newly arrived Beethoven a thing or two on how the big boys played. Soon, however, he found the young Beethoven formidable competition. "Ah, he is no man, he's a devil," declared Gelinek. "He will play me and all of us to death. And how he improvises."

♠ In 1943, the Danish Royal Opera in Copenhagen performed Gershwin's folk opera *Porgy and Bess* 22 times in one season. The Nazi occupiers, having had enough of this Yankee insolence, threatened to blow up the theatre if the show didn't close. The show closed. Meanwhile the Danish Underground used *Porgy* as its symbol of resistance against the Nazis. For a while, every time the Nazis broadcast their victories over the Danish Radio, the Danish Underground interrupted the program with John Bubbles singing "It Ain't Necessarily So."

♠ German poet Goethe, upon hearing the 7-year-old Mozart, put his genius on the level of Shakespeare and Raphael.

♠ On May 1, 1809, with Haydn in the last weeks of his life, the French began a 24-hour artillery barrage of Vienna. When Vienna finally fell, Napoleon had guards placed outside Haydn's home so that the old master could be protected from further discomfort. The noise of the guns shattered Haydn's nerves. In defiance of the French, however, almost every day Haydn went to the piano and played the Austrian National Anthem. He died quietly on May 31, 1809, as Vienna began living under the French. His funeral was almost unnoticed because of the war. On June 15, a memorial was held in his honor. Among others, many high-ranking French officers were in attendance.

♠ "I pay no attention whatever to anybody's praise or blame," said Mozart. "I simply follow my own feelings."

♠ A particularly temperamental prima donna frustrated Toscanini during rehearsals by insisting that she was the star of the show. Having had enough, Toscanini shouted, "Madam, stars are found only in heaven."

♠ "I cannot help it," explained Haydn defending the cheerfulness of his church music. "I give forth what is in me. When I think of the Divine Being, my heart is so full of joy that the notes fly off as if from a spindle. As I have a cheerful heart, He will pardon me if I serve Him cheerfully."

♠ "As for my feelings, I shall never be calculating and politic," said Schubert. "I come straight out with what is in me, and that's that."

♠ While director of the Gewandhaus Orchestra in Leipzig, Mendelssohn fought hard to improve his players' work conditions and pay. When the city tried to raise funds for a monument to Bach, though he revered Bach, Mendelssohn refused to join the campaign until the city assured him that his musicians would be better taken care of.

♠ Richard Strauss was asked whether it was tasteful for a composer to make himself the hero of a symphony as he had in *Ein Heldenleben* (A Hero's Life) and *Symphonia Domestica*. "And why not?" replied Strauss. "I consider myself at least as interesting as Napoleon or Alexander the Great."

♠ Conducting from the piano with wild and broad gestures, Beethoven knocked over a candlestick. The audience laughed and that angered him. Then he had two boys hold candles behind him, and he took it from the top. During the same passage he jumped up with excitement and his arm hit one of the boys in the gut. The boy yelped and dropped the candle. The audience laughed again, angering Beethoven so much that he smashed both hands on the keyboard and broke six strings.

♠ In 1841, the German poet Heinrich Heine said of Liszt: "All pianists pale beside him with the exception of the one and only Chopin, the *Raphael of the Piano*." Heine added, "Indeed, with this one exception, all other pianists heard this year are only pianists who excel by their ability to handle their instrument. With Liszt, however, we no longer think of the conquest of difficulties – the piano vanishes and the music appears."

These stories come from Johann Andreas Schachtner, a trumpeter in the Salzburg court, who was a family friend of the Mozarts:

♠ A group of musicians was playing when the five-year-old Wolfgang picked up a violin and began playing. He had never touched the violin until then. Also, on the day the four-year-old wrote his first keyboard concerto, now lost, his father said, "Look, Herr Schachtner, how correct and orderly it is. Only it could not even be of any use, for it is so extraordinarily difficult that no one in the world can play it." Wolfgang set him straight: "That's just why it is a concerto. It must be practiced until one can play it perfectly."

♠ Beethoven met Goethe in 1812 in Teplitz, Bohemia. While strolling together one afternoon, they encountered the emperor, the empress, Archduke Rudolf, and their entourage. Goethe removed his hat and stepped aside, bowing. Not so Beethoven. He pulled his hat down over his forehead, buttoned up his overcoat and, with his arms folded, marched straight through the group. Archduke Rudolf greeted Beethoven, and all stood aside for him to pass. A few minutes later Beethoven said to Goethe, "There are thousands of princess in the world, but there is only one Beethoven."

♠ After two weeks in England for the Birmingham Festival, Mendelssohn was anxious to get home to his new wife Cecil. He left Birmingham by coach at midday, following a morning concert, and arrived in London about midnight. An hour later he was on a mail coach for Dover, arriving at 9 a.m. With no breakfast, he set sail immediately for Bowline. Arriving without sleep, he took a coach to Cologne through Belgium. From there, the boat trip down the Rhine River ended when the steamer became fogbound. Mendelssohn got off and found a coach, turning up in Koblenz at 3 a.m. Some 12 hours later he arrived in Frankfurt to a waiting Cecil. A three-day coach ride put them in Leipzig just before lunch. That evening Mendelssohn conducted the opening concert of the season with the Gewandhaus Orchestra.

♠ Mozart had an astonishing musical mind. When working on a composition, he could see it clearly in his mind so that by the time he sat to write, the work was already completed in his head. That is why few corrections or alterations exist in his scores.

♠ "I have no ambition to soar like an eagle or a bird of Paradise," said Liszt to his mistress Carolyne Sayn-Wittgenstein, who felt she could push him to accomplish more in life. "I keep quiet here on earth and put my trust in the life to come. I must, therefore, protest humbly and sadly against your misjudgment of me."

♠ Verdi, who was down to earth and shunned publicity, was once asked what he considered his best work. "It's the rest home for aged musicians that I had built in Milan," he said. Another time a friend asked him why he didn't write his memoirs. "It is quite enough that the world has tolerated my music so long," said Verdi. "Never shall I condemn it to read my prose."

And when love speaks, the voices of all the gods makes heaven drowsy with harmony

---

Shakespeare

$\mathcal{I}$n 1957, while waiting at Tehran airport for a flight that would eventually bring my older brother Ramon and me to America, I heard a lovely, lilting waltz on the sound system that would haunt me for years. I looked for it everywhere, but without knowing the title, finding it proved impossible. One day on my radio program, when the recording I was playing had the wrong timing listed and I was left with about seven minutes to fill fast, I grabbed the first CD of waltzes I could find in the music library and cued a piece approximately that length. By Jove I was shocked, for the music was the same pretty waltz I had heard at that airport so long ago. The piece was "Sobre las Olas," also known as "Over the Waves," composed in 1887 by the Mexican composer Juventino Rosas (1868-1894). Rosas, who played violin for road shows, is known to have written "Sobre las Olas" for a certain young lady, but she turned him down. In 1951, Mario Lanza sang the tune, with new lyrics and titled "The Loveliest Night of the Year," in his film The Great Caruso. Being a sucker for stories of love, I came across a bunch from the world of classical music:

♠ Chopin's love affair with the writer George Sand (Aurore Lucille Dupin Dudevant) lasted from 1838 to 1847. Chopin first met Sand in 1836 in Lizst's apartment at the Hotel de France in Paris. He disliked her. In April 1838, he saw her again in the salon of Countess Charlotte Marliani, the wife of the Spanish council in Paris. The next time Chopin and Sand met, however, something sparked between them. Liszt's mistress, the Countess Marie d'Agoult, called it "quite delicious." On one occasion Sand scribbled a note to Chopin. It read: *"On vous adore"* (People adore you.) Sand's friend, the actress Marie Dorval, added the words *"Et moi aussi"* (And so do I.) The note Chopin received from Sand read: *"On vous adore. Et moi aussi"* (Everyone adores you. And so do I.).

♠ "The cello is like a beautiful woman who has not grown older, but younger with time, more slender, more supple, more graceful" – Pablo Casals.

♠ Beethoven had many love affairs. He was romancing a female student on the couch when another student, Ferdinand Ries, walked in on them. Realizing the delicate situation, Ries turned to leave, but Beethoven yelled, "Sit down. Play something." A while later Beethoven yelled again: "Now play something passionate."

♠ At an1851 concert, Gottschalk so dazzled a young lady that at the end of the performance she carried him off the stage to her carriage and drove off. Gottschalk wasn't heard from for five weeks.

♠ Throughout his colorful life, Liszt had many love affairs, mostly with noble women. His first important love was his 17-year-old student, Carolyne de Saint Crique. Her father was the minister of commerce for Charles X. Liszt and Carolyne fell in love and soon her piano lessons stretched well into the night. When her parents discovered the affair, they fired Liszt and sent Carolyne to a convent. Eventually Carolyne married Count d'Arigaux, and Liszt pursued other females.

♠ Jenny Lind, the *Swedish Nightingale*, was deeply in love with Mendelssohn. Even though he found her lovely and exciting, and a joy to be with, nothing happened between them. Mendelssohn was in love with his wife Cecil. Nonetheless Cecil remained leery of Lind. After Mendelssohn's death Jenny Lind mourned him deeply: " … the only person who brought fulfillment to my spirit, and almost as soon as I found him, I lost him again."

♠ In *Don Giovanni*, Leporello sings an aria in which he recites all of Don Giovanni's love affairs. The tally is astounding: Don Giovanni had 1,003 love affairs in Spain, 640 in Italy, 231 in Germany, 100 in France and 91 in Turkey. That's 2,065 love affairs altogether. *A good breakfast will do it every time.*

♠ Handel had sent his cembalo player, Sandoni, to Italy to hire the singer Francesca Cuzzoni, who also happened to be temperamental and headstrong. Sandoni fell in love with the lady and they were married on the way to London. Story has it that later Guzzoni poisoned poor Sandoni.

♠ Liszt, having fathered many illegitimate children, often found himself defending against speculation. He had a standard reply to all these. In the case of the pianist Franz Servais, known to have been his son, Liszt said, "I know his mother by correspondence and one cannot arrange that sort of thing by correspondence."

♠ Modest Mussorgsky hated the institution of marriage, but friends tried to marry him off. He once told Ludmilla Ivanova Shestakinova, composer Mikhail Glinka's sister: "If you ever read in the paper that I shot or hanged myself, it will be because I had got married."

♠ In London in the 1770s, the Polish-born composer and pianist Johann Samuel Schroter asked a wealthy woman named Rebecca to marry him. Her father, however, warned him to stay away from her or he would sue him. The old guy eventually gave in, promising Schroter a financial package only if he forgot about music and lived respectably. Schroter surprised everybody and accepted the offer. In the early 1790s, after Schroter's death, Rebecca chased Haydn, who was in London for a series of concerts, but nothing came of the relationship.

♠ Schumann's last days in high school were filled with music, joy and serenity. In his hometown of Zwickaw he met Karl Carus, a cultured merchant who often hosted musical gatherings in his home. Herr Carus had a nephew, Edward, whose beautiful wife, Agnes, stole Schumann's heart. But she wasn't the only beauty frying his hormones. Now the handsome lad was falling in love as a routine: Liddy Hempel, Nanni Patsch and Ernestine Von Fricken. He waxed reams of love poems to them. In 1834, the 17-year-old beauty Ernestine was studying with Friedrich Wieck, while living in his house. At the time there was nothing between Schumann and Wieck's daughter

Clara. Schumann and Ernestine became engaged. When her father, the Baron Von Fricken, found out about the engagement, he rushed to Leipzig and took his daughter home. Ernestine was illegitimate, her mother being the Countess Zedwitz, and the engagement was broken off by mutual consent.

♠ Schumann fell in love with Clara Wieck when he was 21 years old and she 12. He kissed her when she was 16, in 1835, on the night before she was to depart for a concert tour – they were coming down the stairs when at the bottom Schumann suddenly took her in his arms. Sometime later he saw her again in Zwickaw, his hometown. They kissed again. She was performing in Dresden when Schumann told her he loved her. He was sure her father would welcome him as a son-in-law, but Friedrich Wieck declared that his daughter had a great future as a concert pianist, whereas the 25-year-old Schumann had squandered his life. Clara was in demand, her name a measure of prestige for him, and good money for the rest of his life. Why would he want to destroy this opportunity by allowing her to marry Schumann who, to him, was undisciplined, spoiled, and a rogue? Wieck wanted a wealthy husband for his daughter.

♠ Friedrich Wieck fought the proposed marriage of Clara to Robert Schumann all the way to the highest court. In 1839, Clara, by then a world-famous concert pianist, asked the authorities to override her father's objections to the proposed marriage. Friedrich Wieck blew up and kicked her out of the house. Clara went to her mother's house in Berlin. Then Friedrich began spreading rumors about Clara's shameless behavior, trying his best to destroy her career. Finally he said he would give his consent, but Clara and Schumann had to meet certain conditions. For example, Clara already had made 7,000 thaler, but he insisted she should receive only 4.5 percent of that. The case dragged on, was appealed, and finally the courts decided in favor of Robert Schumann and Clara Wieck. The two were married on September 12, 1839. Years later Friedrich Wieck came around and there was reconciliation. The marriage lasted until Schumann's death in 1856.

♠ Strauss had several wives. Wife No. 2 was so angry when he divorced her and married No. 3 that she picketed his house.

♠ George Philip Telemann's first wife died in childbirth, 15 months after they were married. He had eight children from his second wife, but only two survived. Later, the wife had a scandalous affair with a Swedish officer in Hamburg, where Telemann was music director. She finally left Telemann – and left him with a massive debt.

♠ Tchaikovsky made the mistake of marrying his 28-year-old student Antonina Milyukova. He did not love Antonina, and felt trapped. "She does not frighten me," he wrote a friend. "She is an annoyance." He tried to commit suicide by wading into the icy Moscow River fully clothed, expecting to catch pneumonia, but the attempted suicide failed and his despair grew. Finally he left Antonina. The hurt from the divorce and the bad publicity stretched for years.

♠ When Chopin was dying, Countess Delphine Potocka, a wealthy singer who had always loved him, rushed from Nice to Paris to be with him. "Now I know why God has delayed so long in calling me to Him," said Chopin. "He wanted me to have the pleasure of seeing you once more." Chopin then asked her to sing for him.

♠ Mendelssohn loved his wife Cecil and showered her with gifts. One gift was a bit unusual. Cecil loved Chopin's music, so Mendelssohn cajoled Chopin into writing a few bars of music especially for her and autographing them.

♠ Schubert had a number of loves. None, however, came near to his love for one of his students, the Countess Karoline Esterhazy. She knew he loved her, but nothing happened. They came from different worlds: one was nobility and the other artist.

♠ In his early days, Emil Waldteufel, the composer of wonderful waltzes, worked as a pianist in a piano factory. One day he heard a lovely voice coming from a nearby window. It was a woman singing, so he accompanied her on the piano. Soon they met and were married, in 1868.

♠ Beethoven was never married. Early on in Bonn, he proposed to Magdalena Willmann, a singer, but she turned him down, declaring he was ugly and a little crazy.

♠ When Dietrich Buxtehude decided to retire as chief organist for the city of Lubeck, Handel applied for the job. The only problem was that to get the job, you had to marry Buxtehude's ugly daughter. Well, one look at the girl, Handel told Buxtehude to keep the job. Eventually a man named Schieferdecker got the gig. *We can assume he got the girl, too.*

♠ Mozart was running around the hallways at *Schoenbrunn* Palace in Vienna when he slipped and fell. Marie Antoinette, Queen Maria Theresa's daughter, helped him up and cleaned the scratch on his knee. Mozart fell in love with her instantly, so goes the story, and asked her to marry him. They were both seven years old.

♠ In 1902, and the French pianist and composer Cecil Chaminade was madly in love with a flutist, but he broke her heart and married another. Still, Chaminade presented him with her flute concertino on his wedding day.

♠ By age 16, Liszt was a depressed musical genius consumed with religion. His father took him to Italy to lift his spirit, and it worked, but sadly, his father caught typhoid fever and died in Bologna, in 1827. Liszt's father had told him something that was to come true: "You have a good heart and a world of intelligence, but women will bring you a great deal of turmoil and conflict in your life." At the time, Liszt had found the prediction strange, admitting he knew nothing about women. In confession, he asked the priest to explain to him the Sixth and the Ninth Commandments, fearing he might have broken them without knowing.

♠ Unlike Beethoven who looked for love among the aristocracy, Mozart courted women of simple background. "The last thing I want is a rich wife," he said. The woman he did marry, Constanza Weber, was anything but rich. He had been in love with her sister, but she married another. Mozart told his father that Constanza was not ugly, but that she was far from beautiful, her whole beauty consisting of two little black eyes and a pretty figure. Later he said he loved her and that she loved him.

♠ One of Tchaikovsky's early loves was Desiree Artot, the daughter of a Belgian horn player. He fell in love with her when she performed in Moscow with a touring Italian company. They talked of marriage, but friends discouraged him, as did his mother. Eventually Artot married a Spanish baritone in Warsaw. Tchaikovsky's friends, breathing a sigh of relief, thought he was more in love with the idea of the singer rather than the woman, and that she, too, was more in love with the composer rather than the man.

♠ Toscanini loved everything about women: the games, the courtship and the ceremonies. He once wrote: "When I was very young, I kissed my first woman and smoked my first cigarette on the same day and, believe me, never since have I wasted any more time on tobacco."

♠ Haydn was never a ladies man, even with a bad marriage. Still, he did manage a few relationships. In England, he met Mrs. Rebecca Schroter, the widow of the Polish-born pianist and composer Johann Samuel Schroter. Haydn told a friend that had he been single, he would have married Rebecca. Another love was Luigia Polzelli, a singer from his early years as music director for Count Esterhazy. Later Polzelli moved to Italy. Haydn also loved Marienne Von Genzinger, who lived in Vienna, and her untimely death broke his heart. He wrote long letters to all of them.

♠ "Immortal Mozart!" wrote philosopher Soren Kierkegaard. "I owe you everything. I have you to thank that I did not die without having loved."

♠ Liszt met Princess Carolyne Sayn-Wittgenstein, who was married to a boring but wealthy man, while on tour in Kiev, Russia, in 1847. He found her attractive and exotic, but most of all, wealthy – she had 30,000 serfs working on her estate in the Ukraine. In the end she left her husband and joined Liszt in Weimar. They had three children together, including Cosima, who later was to dump her husband, the renowned pianist and conductor Hans Von Bulow, and marry Richard Wagner. The Czar refused Carolyne's divorce and confiscated all of her estate at Woronince. She disobeyed orders to return to Russia and became an exile.

♠ Dvorak's first love was Josefa Cermak. She rejected him, so he married her sister Anna. Similarly, Mozart loved Aloysia Weber, who turned him down, and he married her sister Constanza. Haydn, too, married the sister of the woman who rejected him. Mozart and Dvorak had good marriages, but Haydn's was a disaster. *I don't know where I'm going with all this.*

♠ Berlioz's love for Shakespeare led him to Harriet Smithson, who was on tour in Paris with an English theatre company. He wrote her many love letters before they met. Harriet thought him a freak and was afraid of him at first, but he won her heart through extraordinary measures. He staged a suicide with an overdose of opium. The attempt failed and he ended up sick for three days. Then he threatened to go to Germany if she didn't marry him. Berlioz and Harriet Smithson were finally married on Oct. 3, 1833.

♠Mendelssohn's aunt Dorothea scandalized the family by marrying the poet Friedrich Von Schlegel. He was much younger, and became her second husband after a long love affair.

♠ Mrs. Gounod, who wanted her husband well dressed, gave him a handsome formal suit with rare buttons. Gounod, in an afternoon tryst with a certain countess, lost one of the buttons. The countess kept it as a souvenir in the form of a locket. Some time later, while having tea with the countess, Mrs. Gounod noticed the locket with the distinct button. "How beautiful," she said. "May I see inside?" *Oy, vey.*

♠ While music director for Count Ferdinand Maximilian Von Morzin, Haydn fell in love with one of his students. Therese Keller's father was a hairdresser, and her brother had been a violinist at St. Stephens Cathedral in Vienna where Haydn sang in his youth. Therese did not love Haydn and instead chose to enter the St.

Nicholas Convent in Vienna. For some odd reason, in 1760, Haydn married her sister Maria Anna, three years his senior – and it became a marriage from hell. Maria Anna was bad-tempered and disliked music. According Haydn's musicians, she often irritated him out of spite by lining her cupboard shelves with his manuscripts. Haydn completely neglected her. He said his single biggest mistake was his marriage. They were separated for a long time. A friend once inquired about a big pile of unopened letters on Haydn's desk. "Oh, they are from my wife," explained Haydn. "She writes me monthly, and I answer her monthly, but I do not open her letters and I am sure she does not open mine."

♠ "As for love, I regard her as the prima donna par excellence, the goddess who sings cavatinas to the brain, intoxicates the ear, and delights the heart." – Rossini.

♠ In 1862, after some years of living and performing in Cuba and the West Indies, Gottschalk returned to America and resumed his concert performances. Many love affairs later, his involvement with a student at the Oakland Female Seminary got him into trouble and he fled to South America.

♠ Franz Liszt had many love affairs, including one with Countess d'Agoult, which began in 1835, when she left her husband and ran away to Switzerland with Liszt. They had three children, of whom only Cosima survived. She married Liszt's student, the renowned pianist and conductor Hanz Von Bulow, later dumping him for Richard Wagner. Liszt's love affair with Countess d'Agoult ended in 1844. She returned to Paris and wrote the novel *Nelida*, under the pen name of Daniel Stern. The book ripped Liszt.

♠ Beethoven loved beautiful women. He wrote a friend to look for a wife for him, specifying that she had to be beautiful. "For it is impossible for me to love anything that is not beautiful," he added, "or else I should have to love myself."

♠ The Irish composer and pianist John Field boasted to a group of ladies that the only reason he married one of his students was because she never paid him and that he knew she never would.

♠ Hector Berlioz was engaged to Marie Felicite Dennis Moke, a piano teacher with a taste for big, strong cigars. In 1830, he won the Prix de Rome prize for composition and went to Italy for a year to study. Before long he heard Marie had decided to marry someone else. Angry and jealous, he tried to drown himself and failed. Then he made plans to murder her. He bought a chambermaid's dress, a pair of pistols, and two bottles of poison, intent on entering her house in disguise and whacking her. Well, now, he took the coach to Paris, but it was the wrong coach and he ended up in Genoa. Worst, he left his disguise on the coach. Hurriedly, he had a seamstress sew him a new disguise and then he took another coach to Paris. That coach went to Nice instead. By then, having had enough, he decided to forget the whole thing, and Marie along with it. He sold the pistols and took to wandering, until the police took him for a vagrant and ran him out of town.

♠ One of Franz Liszt's love affairs was with Princess Carolyne Sayn-Wittgenstein, who also served as his literary ghostwriter. The princess, a religious fanatic, adopted a masculine lifestyle years after their breakup. She liked smoking big cigars.

♠ Beethoven's *Immortal Beloved* is the subject of a love letter he wrote in 1812. To whom he wrote it is a mystery. Much speculation covers the subject. Could it have been Dorothea Von Ertmann, a student? Josephine Von Brunsvik, for whom he wrote the *Appassionata* Sonata? Giulietta Giucciardi, to whom he dedicated the *Moonlight* Sonata? Or the 15-year-old Theresa Malfatti? It's a big question. The letter opens thusly: "My angel, my all, my very self ..."

♠ Pauline Plater, the Polish countess who lived in Paris and knew the composer and pianists Franz Liszt, Ferdinand Hiller and Frederyk Chopin, once told Chopin, "If I were young and pretty, my little Chopin, I would take you for a husband, Hiller for a friend and Liszt for a lover."

Pardon my acid

$\mathcal{M}$y late aunt Lola, whom I loved dearly, had an acerbic sense of humor that often left me doubled over with laughter. Toward the end of her life in the late 1990s, although nearly blind from diabetes, she still retained her old spirit. I was morning drive announcer at WNIB radio in Chicago, and spent many afternoons with my aunt chatting over tea. She once recalled, laughing, that long ago my grandmother Sonja had told her, "Daughter, no matter what happens in your life, your big mouth will help you make it through." The stories in this section of OBIE'S OPUS make me realize how much I miss that mouth and that delicious sense of humor.

♠ A high society lady in Chicago invited Fritz Kreisler to play at her party. She asked his fee. He said $3,000. She accepted, adding, "But of course, it is understood that you will refrain from mixing with my guests." Kreisler wrote back, "In that case, madam, the fee will be only $2,000."

♠ A newspaper in Arkansas, unimpressed with Enrico Caruso, could not understand why a great pitcher like Walter Johnson got only $600 a game, while "Caruso, the Italian singer, gets $3,000 a night for standing on the stage and screeching so no one but her own race knows what she says."

♠ Rossini marked errors on student papers with crosses. He once sent a manuscript back to a student with a few markings. "I'm so happy there are so few mistakes," the kid beamed. Looking stern, Rossini said, "If I had marked all the errors in the music with crosses, your score would be a cemetery."

♠ The Leipzig Gewandhaus Orchestra criticized Brahms the first time it played his Piano Concerto No. 1. Later, a director asked, "Whither are you going to lead us tonight, Mr. Brahms, to Heaven?" Brahms said, "It's all the same to me which direction you go."

♠ Some cry for Haydn, some Mozart,
Just as the whim bites, for my part,
I do not care a farthing candle,
For either of them – or for Handle
– Charles Lamb

♠ "A vile beastly rottenheaded foolbegotten brazenthroated pernicious piggish screaming, tearing, roaring, perplexing, splitmecrackle, crashmecriggle insane ass of a woman is practicing howling below-stairs with a brute of a singmaster so horribly that my head is nearly off" – British humorist Edward Lear (1812-1888) complaining about his neighbor.

♠ Mischa Elman, like Rodney Dangerfield, sometimes got no respect. His son, who was studying the violin, once played for an intimate group of Elman's friends. "He's wonderful," a lady said to Elman. "I'm sure he'll grow up to be another Heifetz."

♠ Josef Hoffman was giving a recital and the doorman wouldn't let this drunk into the concert hall. "Look here," said the drunk, "you don't suppose I would go to a piano recital unless I was drunk?"

♠ Luigi Cherubini, attending Jacques Halevy's opera, was silent until after the second act, when Halevy asked him, "Maestro, have you nothing to say to me?" Cherubini snarled. "I have been listening to your music for two hours and you have said nothing to me."

♠ An autograph collector asked Mischa Elman for three autographs. "But why three?" wondered Elman. "Because I can trade three of your autographs for one of Heifetz's," said the collector.

♠ "How wonderful opera would be if there were no singers" – Rossini.

♠ For Camille Saint-Saens, conductors came in two types: those who took music too fast and those who took it too slow. A young conductor once wrote and asked him what tempo he would suggest for the finale of the second symphony. "Dear Sir," Saint-Saens wrote back, "the right tempo is ONE-two, ONE-two. Faithfully yours, Saint-Saens."

♠ The Can-Can was described in 1938 by the Oxford Companion to Music as a "boisterous and latterly indecorous dance, of the quadrille order, dating from 1840, and then exploited in Paris for the benefit of such British and American visitors as were willing to pay well to be well shocked." The source concluded by saying, "Its exact nature is unknown to anyone connected with this encyclopedia."

♠ In 1723, the position of cantor at St. Thomas Church in Leipzig was offered to Telemann, music director at Hamburg, but he turned it down. Christoph Graupner, music director at Darmstadt, turned down the offer, too. Johann Sebastian Bach was the third choice, prompting city councilman Platz to say, "Since the best man could not be obtained, a mediocre one would have to be accepted."

♠ Countess Marie d'Agoult, Liszt's mistress, was born in 1805, the daughter of Vicomte de Flavigny, a French émigré. Even though she was bohemian in her lifestyle and thought, she still managed to float in high society. A writer described her as "six inches of snow covering twenty feet of lava." *She was perfect for Liszt.*

♠ In 1842, Gottschalk tried to enroll at the Paris Conservatory, but, Pierre Zimmerman, a famous piano teacher there, blocked his way. (Zimmerman was Charles Gounod's father-in-law.) Zimmerman claimed no pianist of quality could come from America, a land of savages and steam engines. *Well, excuse me!*

♠ "There is something sad about the sound of the clarinet, even if it plays a merry tune," said the Belgian opera composer Andre Modest Gretry. "If I were to dance in prison, I should wish to do so to the accompaniment of a clarinet."

♠ A young opera composer asked Giuseppe Verdi for advice, showing him a scene and going into a lengthy explanation about how he would put it to music. "Is that what you, too, would do with that, master?" he asked, then. "No," said Verdi. "I would just sit down and write a little music."

♠ George Bizet's teacher wrote a letter of introduction to a friend, the composer Saverio Mercadante. "He is a wholly enchanting and a delightful young man, intelligent, congenial, well-mannered and sociable," he said. "I am quite sure you will like him immensely. P.S., Bizet hasn't got the slightest trace of any musical talent." *Bizet somehow managed to compose the opera Carmen.*

♠ The church refused to sanctify Liszt's marriage to Princess Carolyne Sayn-Wittgenstein, causing them to break up and driving Liszt into a monastic life. In 1865, he joined the order of St. Francis and was given the title of Abbe. He said he had not changed except to simplify his life, but people saw the move as a publicity stunt, to which Liszt was no stranger. Hearing Liszt's confession, the priest remarked, "Basta, caro Liszt! Go tell the rest of your sins to the piano."

♠ A soprano, rehearsing with an orchestra, couldn't hit the high notes. Finally the frustrated conductor said, "Madam, I fear that we are not together. Will you please give the orchestra your A?"

♠ Koussevitzky was rehearsing the Boston Symphony when he abruptly stopped, dissatisfied with a particular musician. "Don't play like an old man," he said. "You're an old man yourself," the musician shot back. "I know that," said Koussevitzky, "but when I conduct like an old man, I will give up the job."

♠ From England, Chopin wrote to a friend: "I have not yet played to any English woman without her saying to me, 'Like water.'" Chopin was critical of English pianists. "They all look at their hands," he said, "and play the wrong notes with much feeling." Chopin added, "Every creature here seems to have a screw loose. Eccentric people, God help them."

♠ Ambrose Bierce described the flute as "A variously perforated hollow stick intended for the punishment of sin, the minister of retribution being commonly a young man with straw-colored eyes and lean hair."

♠ Beethoven had a friend named Stricher, whose daughter one day was practicing Beethoven's "Variations in C Minor" on the piano.

"By whom is that?" Beethoven asked. "By you," said the girl. "Such nonsense by me," declared Beethoven. "O, Beethoven, what an ass you are."

♠ Italian-American oboist Bruno Labate, tired of Otto Klemperer's harping on the fine points of intonation and phrasing during the rehearsal, barked from his orchestra seat, "Dr. Kemps, you talka' too much." Later, a colleague told Labate he would be scared to say something like that to Klemperer. Labate shrugged. "I got seventy-five thousand dollar in the bank. I no get scared."

♠ A conductor, prone to long and rhapsodic lectures to his musicians, on one occasion stopped rehearsals to explain what he wanted: "The music should sound as if you were playing on top of a high mountain, overlooking a bank of clouds. You are fanned by the winds …" He went on and on. Finally the concertmaster had enough. "Look," he said. "Just tell us whether you want it played loud or soft."

♠ Schubert submitted his famous song "Erlkonig" (Earl King) to the publisher *Breitkoff and Hartel*, who rejected it and returned it, by mistake, to a certain Franz Schubert living in Dresden. The Dresden Schubert was insulted that this young upstart from Vienna would dare call himself Franz Schubert. He wrote back to the publishers, saying in part, "I'll keep it to find out who sends you this trash."

♠ Writer and satirist Ambrose Bierce described the clarinet as "An instrument of torture operated by a person with cotton in his ears. There are two instruments that are worse than a clarinet – two clarinets."

♠ At one time Tchaikovsky disliked all things English. "Dickens and Thackeray are the only people I forgive for being English," he declared, while discounting Shakespeare for being too distant in history.

♠ Cherubini, who met Beethoven in Vienna in 1805, was asked what he thought of the master's music. "It makes me sneeze," he said.

♠ A young lady journalist interviewing Heifetz asked, "Now, Mr. Heifetz, how do you spell your name?" Heifetz was shocked, since he was famous, but nonetheless spelled his name. He watched her write it down. Giving her an icy look, he then said, "Aren't you going to ask me what I do? I play the fiddle."

More than any composer I know of, Wagner has inspired peppery tongues:

♠ Mark Twain preferred to be anywhere but at a Wagner opera. "There isn't often anything in a Wagner opera that one could call by such a violent thing as acting," he said. "As a rule, all you would see would be a couple of people, one of them standing still, and the other catching flies."

♠ "I like Wagner's operas better than anyone's," said Oscar Wilde. "You can talk the whole time without anyone hearing what you're saying."

♠ "Wagner has beautiful moments but awful quarter hours" – Rossini.

♠ "I love Wagner, but the music I prefer is that of a cat hung up by the tail outside a window, and trying to stick to glass with its claws," said French poet Charles Baudelaire. "There is an odd grating on the glass which I find at the same time strange, irritating, and singularly harmonious."

♠ "Wagner's music is better than it sounds" – Mark Twain.

♠ "The typical Wagnerian soprano looks like an ox, moves like a carthorse, and sounds like a haystack" – music writer Ernest Newman.

♠ "The opera was *Parsifal* – and I enjoyed it in spite of the singing" – Mark Twain.

♠ Auber asked Rossini if he had liked the performance of Wagner's *Tannhauser*. "It is music one must hear several times," said Rossini, "and I'm not going again."

♠ A friend stopped by Rossini's house in Paris and was surprised to find a score of Wagner's opera *Tannhauser* on the piano – upside down. He tried to put the score right side up and Rossini stopped him. "I already played it right side up, but could make nothing of it," he said. "Then I tried it the other way, and it sounds much better."

All right, enough. Let's give the poor guy a break.

♠ "What I love about jazz is that it's blue and you don't care" – Eric Satie.

♠ Hans Knapertsbusch rejected fashion and always conducted with a score. When asked about it, he said, "Yes, I use the score, and why not? I can read music."

♠ In 1917, violinist Mischa Elman and pianist Leopold Godowsky were in the audience when Jascha Heifetz made his Carnegie Hall debut. It was a tropical night. "Terribly hot, isn't it?" complained Elman, mopping his brow. "Not for pianists," Godowsky answered.

♠ At a Beethoven symphony concert, Berlioz sat crying. A friend said, "You seem to be greatly affected, *monsieur*. Had you not better retire for a while?" Berlioz replied, "Are you under the impression that I am here to enjoy myself?"

♠ "A genius naturally can do without taste, for example Beethoven," said Claude Debussy. "But Mozart, his equal in genius, has, in addition, the most delicate taste."

♠ A conductor, known for his tantrums, was particularly critical of a player. Finally, having had enough, the player stopped the conductor. "Look, buddy," he said. "If you keep on like that, I'm going to follow your beat."

♠ Ignacy Paderewski was playing piano in a salon in Paris and felt a draft on his back. He begged the hostess to close the window, adding, "Surely, you can't expect to enjoy two pleasures at the same time – listening to an artist and killing him."

♠ Brahms was asked why he had grown that patriarchal beard he was so proud of. Brahms replied, "I'm competing with Michelangelo's *Moses*."

♠ When composer Giacomo Meyerbeer died, his nephew, while visiting Rossini, insisted on playing the march he had written for his uncle's funeral. Rossini listened to it. "Very nice," he said, "but wouldn't it have been much better if you had died and your uncle had composed the march?"

♠ Franz Liszt played a new composition for Rossini. "I prefer the other one," said Rossini in the end. "Which one?" Liszt was puzzled. "The chaos in Haydn's *Creation*," said Rossini.

♠ Paderewski was a pianist, composer, writer and politician. During the Versailles Peace Conference, Clemenceau, the world-renowned politician, told him, "So you abandoned your musical career to become a politician. What a come-down."

♠ At the Paris Conservatory, his teacher asked Berlioz, "Why do you include a two-measure rest in this passage?" Berlioz explained that he wanted an effect produced by silence. "Good," said the teacher. "Suppress the rest of the piece. The effect will be better still."

♠ After a concert, a society lady asked Paderewski what he had played. "A Beethoven sonata," he said. "Oh, is he still composing?" she asked. "No, Madam," Paderewski replied, "at the moment he is decomposing."

"If a man tells me he likes Mozart, I know in advance that he is a bad musician" – Frederick Delius.

♠ Luigi Cherubini, the famous composer of operas, as well as the director of the Paris Conservatory, was autocratic, bad-tempered and intolerant, a bureaucrat who went strictly by the book. When Adolph Adam, composer of the ballet *Giselle*, was presented to him as a young boy, Cherubini is reputed to have remarked, "My! What an ugly child."

♠ A young composer was complaining to Brahms that publication of his new composition was being held up. "Patience, young man," advised Brahms. "You can afford not to be immortal for a few more years."

♠ After conducting a performance of one of his own works, Ralph Vaughan Williams stepped off the podium, muttering, "If that's modern music, I don't like it."

♠ Rossini was asked by a young composer to listen to two original pieces he had written. After listening to the first one, Rossini said, "I like the other one better."

♠ A Viennese said to Brahms, "Your new symphony is very good, but it reminds me of other music." Brahms was puzzled. "What other music?" he asked. "Your next symphony," said the Viennese.

♠ When Koussevitzky, who was also a virtuoso bassist, became conductor of the Boston Symphony, the bass section asked him to play. Many of the players attended the performance, including a cellist, who later said, "It was astounding. Never have I heard such bass playing. I closed my eyes and said to myself, 'That is not a bass. It sounds like a lousy bass.'"

♠ Composer Luigi Dallapicola said Vivaldi had not written 450 concerti, but had written one concerto 450 times.

♠ During rehearsals of an opera, the tenor failed to deliver what Leonard Bernstein asked for. "I know it's the historical prerogative of the tenor to be stupid," declared Bernstein, "but you, sir, have abused that privilege."

♠ Brahms and a friend were strolling by a house in Vienna with a commemorative plaque on it. "The day I die they'll put a sign in front of my house, too," said Brahms. Replied his friend, "Of course, and it will read, 'House to let.'"

♠ A young composer brought Rossini a funeral march he had composed in honor of Beethoven. After glancing at the first page, Rossini nodded and said, "I would much rather be looking at a Beethoven funeral march written in your honor."

♠ In Puccini's opera *La Boheme*, Mimi with her chilled hands has been the butt of many pranks. Enrico Caruso once passed a hot potato into the hands of the soprano singing the part opposite him. And the American tenor Frederick Jagel, as Rodolfo, once slipped a warm sausage in the muff that Musetta gives to Mimi.

♠ Borodin was called as an expert witness in the case of two young composers who accused each other of plagiarism. After the compositions were played, the judge asked Borodin what he thought. Who was the injured party? Borodin replied, "My good friend Mussorgsky."

♠ In Paris, the young Mendelssohn thought that although Liszt played well and had splendid fingers, he was brainless. He called Rossini "The great maestro windbag." Meyerbeer didn't impress him, especially after his lecture on the nature of the French horn. "I laughed so much I nearly fell off the chair," later said Mendelssohn. Worst, when told that he resembled Meyerbeer, Mendelssohn got a haircut and combed his hair differently. *No way!*

♠ Jascha Heifetz, reminiscing about the old days with Harpo Marx, said he had been earning a living since age six. Said Harpo, "What were you before then, a bum?"

♠ Brahms hated coffee with chicory. After a long day's walk in the woods once, he and a friend stopped at a café and were served coffee with chicory. "My dear old lady," said Brahms to the owner. "Have you some chicory?" She said she had. "It's not possible," declared Brahms. "May I see it?" The old woman brought him two packages of chicory. "Is that all you have?" asked Brahms. That was all. "Well now," he said, pocketing the packages, "you can go back and make us some black coffee."

♠ After hearing "Pavane for a Dead Princess" performed poorly, Maurice Ravel said to the pianist, "Pardon me, it is the princess who is dead, not the Pavane."

♠ Feodor Chaliapin was asked to sing at noon. It was the wrong thing to say to the great singer. "Sing at noon, Madam?" he said. "At noon I am happy to be able to spit."

♠ Brahms, preparing to leave a party, put on his coat and announced, "If through oversight I neglected to insult anyone among those present, I apologize to him."

♠ Fritz Kreisler was invited to dinner. The note also read: "P.S. Please bring your violin." Kreisler wrote back, accepting, but added, "P.S. My violin never dines out."

♠ Asked by his friend Dmitri Shostakovich what he thought of Puccini, Benjamin Britten said, "His operas are dreadful." Shostakovich replied, "No, Ben, you're wrong. He wrote marvelous operas but dreadful music."

♠ Thomas Augustine Arne (1710-1778), the composer of "Rule Britannia," was asked to judge a contest between two singers who had about as much talent as a slug. After hearing these two characters croak, Arne said to one, "You are the worst singer I have ever heard in my life." The other singer jumped with joy. "Then I win." Arne shook his head and declared, "No, you can't sing at all."

♠ Ambrose Bierce, the American writer and satirist, called the piano "A parlor utensil for subduing the impenitent visitor," adding, "It is operated by depressing the keys of the machine and the spirits of the audience."

♠ In 1927 in Paris, after Vladimir Horowitz had finished playing Ravel's "Jex D'eau," a man sat next to him and said, "You play that as if it were composed by Franz Liszt. Here we play it as if it were composed by Maurice Ravel." The man was Maurice Ravel.

♠ "Tell me, Herr Doktor," an admirer asked Brahms, "how do you write the slow movements of your symphonies, these glorious pieces of celestial beauty?" Brahms replied, "Quite simple, dear lady, quite simple. You see, my publishers order them like that."

♠ "A confounded box of whistles" – a description of the organ by Sir Christopher Wren, the architect of London's St. Paul's Cathedral.

♠ Oscar Levant was asked what made a successful piano virtuoso. "Five essential things are required," he said. "Talent, imagination, energy, determination – and a very rich wife."

♠ "Going to the opera, like getting drunk, is a sin that carries its own punishment" – Hannah More.

♠ Brahms, playing a Beethoven sonata with a cellist, kept stepping a little too hard on the pedal on the piano. Finally the frustrated cellist said, "Softer, I can't hear my cello." Brahms shrugged and said, "You're lucky. I can."

♠ "Swans sing before they die," said the English poet Samuel Taylor Coleridge. "'Twere no bad thing should certain persons die before they sing."

♠ A singer asked Brahms for some of his least known songs for her concert. "Take some of my posthumous ones," said Brahms. "No one will ever know them."

♠ The baroque composer Jean Philippe Rameau lay dying while a priest chanted his prayers incessantly. Finally Rameau breathed hard, opened his eyes, shook his head, and with a slight smile uttered his last words: "I say, my dear Abbe, how can you sing so atrociously out of tune?"

♠ A singer was giving a recital in Italy. Following an aria, somebody in the audience shouted, "*Bis . . . Encore.*" The man sang it again. Just before the third encore, a voice from the balcony yelled, "You're going to keep singing it until you get it right."

♠ "What beautiful music paper you use" – Brahms' evaluation of a symphony by a young composer.

♠ In 1876, Cambridge University wanted to give Brahms an honorary Ph.D. He was delighted, until Clara Schumann told him that he had to accept the honor in person – in England. She warned that the crossing of the English Channel was horrible, but worst, that he had to dress formally for the occasion. Forget it, Brahms said. He liked the English, but he said, "You have to live in a dress suit there."

♠ While rehearsing his opera *Les Paladin*, Rameau told one performer to take a certain aria much faster. "But if I sing it so fast, the public will not be able to hear the words," said the singer. "That doesn't matter," said Rameau. "I only want them to hear my music."

♠ Brahms served one season as director of Vienna's *Singakademie*. Although his programming was respected, everyone became weary of its usually dark tone. The joke was: "When Brahms is in really high spirit, he gets us to sing 'The Grave is My Joy.'"

Sometimes nothing you do makes a difference

*M*y listeners, bless their hearts, were delightful, except for a handful that complained habitually. After a while I realized there was no pleasing some people. Liszt put it differently, but the message is the same: Liszt generally wore the same type of clothing without heeding the weather. "Why should I take notice of the weather if it insists upon disregarding me?" he said.

♠ When the German composer Karl Friedrich Abel (*Aw-bel*) (1723-1787) arrived in England, people called him Abel (*Ay-bel*). Hard as he tried to correct the pronunciation, he got nowhere, so he changed the name to Ibel (*Ee-bel*). People then started calling him Ibel (*Eye-bel*). He finally gave up and returned to the original Abel (*Aw-bel*).

♠ "He has never learned anything and he'll never get anywhere" – Beethoven's teacher Albrechtsberger.

♠ Venezuelan pianist Teresa Carreno, renowned in her own right, was the third wife of the composer and piano superstar Eugene D'Albert's six wives. A promoter once advertised her concert this way: "Eugene d'Albert's First Concerto will be played on the second of March by his third wife." *Thank you.*

♠ In Milan in 1832, while attending Donizetti's opera *L'Elisir d' amore*, Berlioz found the audience unruly – talking, gambling, eating. Judging from their huge open mouths, he thought the singers competed to see who could shout the loudest. He left frustrated. People tried to convince him that Italians occasionally did listen, but he said he'd rather work in a spice house in Paris than write an opera for the Italians.

♠ Modest Mussorgsky was one of those people who start something and don't finish it. Friends once offered him 80 rubles if he would finish his opera *The Fair at Sorochinsk*. Others offered to pay him 100 rubles a month if he would promise to finish *Khovanchina*. He finished neither.

♠ A conductor, who preferred soft, almost hushed sounds, was rehearsing an orchestra when he kept asking the French horn section to play softly. The horn players finally had enough of this softly business, so on cue from the section leader, they held the horns to their mouths and pretended to play. "Splendid," said the conductor. "Now just a wee bit softer and you'll have it."

♠ Beethoven was ill, so his friend Stephan Von Breuning took him to his home to nurse. After Beethoven recovered, he flew into a range and wouldn't forgive his friend. It seems Herr Breuning had forgotten to inform the landlord of Beethoven's time away from his apartment and Beethoven had to pay back rent.

♠ Without realizing, Toscanini frequently sang along while conducting – in a raucous, high-pitched tone. On one occasion he stopped the rehearsal and demanded, "Who is making that noise?"

♠ Autograph collectors hounded Brahms, but he ignored them. So they devised ways to acquire his signature. For instance, one demanded payment for "ten dozen rapiers." Another ordered one of his Viennese piano sonatas. The idea was to have Brahms refuse in writing, in which case the letter would bear his signature.

♠ Richard Wagner disliked Brahms, because, among other reasons, he said Brahms cost him a friend – Friedrich Nietzsche. While visiting Wagner, Nietzsche insisted Wagner play a Brahms song that he, Nietzsche, had brought along. Another night Nietzsche took the same song to Wagner and insisted on hearing it again. "You've got to know the music," declared Nietzsche. "You must change your view of Brahms. He is a great master, the true successor to Beethoven." That apparently did it for Wagner and he threw Nietzsche out of the house.

♠ In 1720, Vivaldi met a young singer in Venice named Anna Giraud. She and her sister moved in with him. Since Vivaldi was a priest, though non-practicing, this arrangement created controversy. Vivaldi insisted Anna Giraud was his housekeeper and a good friend, but some believed there was more to it. No one knows. In 1741, when Vivaldi died in Vienna, Giraud returned to Venice, living until 1750.

Wait till you're fifty and you'll see

Or trying to make sense out of life

*A*t age 22, all of life's answers were as simple as coffee with cigarettes. I remember spending hours in coffee shops with friends discussing everything from Spinoza to Fellini. We understood everything, of course, and had the right answers to all the wrongs in the world. As I grew older, I came to know and understand less and less. Then sometime around age 50, I came across the French composer Eric Satie's thoughts on aging and realized my dilemma. "When I was young," he said, "people used to say to me wait until you're fifty, you'll see. I am fifty," he said. "I still haven't seen anything." At age 65, I still wrestle with the same dilemma – I have no idea what the hell's going on with life. Maybe when I reach 100, I might figure the whole thing out. In the meantime, I have tried to look for some of the answers in the following stories.

♠ As a boy in Bonn, Germany, Beethoven frequently looked sloppy in appearance. Frau Cacilia Fischer, a neighbor, once told him, "How dirty you look. You should be tidier." Beethoven shot back, "What difference does it make? When I become a gentleman, no one will notice."

♠ The conductor thought the orchestra's cello section was out of tune. He stopped rehearsals intent on personally tuning every cello. Well, as each cellist came out of the conductor's dressing room, he handed the same cello to the next player to take in, about a dozen or so, and the maestro kept tuning the same cello. When he was finished, he resumed rehearsals, admitting the cello section sounded perfect.

♠ Much has been made of Beethoven's *Eroica* Symphony: what it is, what the title means, who gets the dedication, and so on. The conductor Arturo Toscanini dismissed all such talk. "Some say this is Napoleon, some Hitler, some Mussolini," he said. "Bah! For me, it's simply allegro con brio."

♠ "You might live in paradise if you would accept life in all its simplicity and soberness, and keep your demand within reasonable limits" – Robert Schumann.

♠ Writer William Saroyan was asked why he wrote so much on the same theme. So he told this story about his uncle, a cellist, who played only one note. His wife, sick of hearing that same note, asked him to play something else. "You know all those cellists who bend over their instruments, their hands running wild all over the fingerboards – do you know what they're doing?" said Uncle Saroyan. "They are looking for the right note. Well, I found the right note – and I'm sticking to it."

♠ "I accept life unconditionally," said pianist Artur Rubinstein. "Most people ask for happiness on condition. Happiness can only be felt if you don't set any conditions."

♠ Opera star Amelita Galli-Curci had a tendency to sing out of tune. She once was asked why she let herself sing out of tune so often. Galli-Curci replied, "Why should I learn to sing in tune when I have made millions singing out of tune?"

♠ "You've got your diet all wrong," Richard Tucker told an aspiring artist. "You've got to learn Mozart before you try Verdi. Put the milk before the meat."

♠ In 1793, when Haydn returned from England to Vienna, his wife insisted that he buy a house. Although they were married on paper only, Haydn bought the house, knowing she would not live in it – and she didn't.

♠ Liszt remained a showman to the end in everything he did. He wrote a long and complimentary piece on Clara Schumann. She liked it, but also said, "What made you say I practiced with a black cat on each side of the pianoforte desk? You know it isn't true." Liszt said, "My dear, Madam, in order to make an article like that go down with the French public it must have something piquant about it."

♠ Rossini told friends he would have preferred to be a cook than a composer.

♠ Beethoven, who loved bread soup, fired his housekeeper for telling him a lie. The friend who had found him the housekeeper asked the reason. "Anyone who tells a lie has not a pure heart and cannot make pure soup," replied Beethoven.

♠ Later in life Rossini was often ill. He was an insomniac, a hypochondriac, and since he loved to eat, he suffered from frequent upset stomachs. "I have all of women's ills," he once told a friend. "All that I lack is the uterus."

♠ Emperor Josef II cared little for Mozart's opera *Don Giovanni*, though he admitted that it was a work of art. "The opera is divine," he told a friend of Mozart's. "I should even venture that it is more beautiful than *Figaro*. But do you know why? Neither you nor I have so good an idea."

♠ Rossini wrote *William Tell* at the height of his career and then retired. He was asked about that. "I wrote operas when melodies overwhelmed me, when they came searching for me," he said. "But one day I noticed that they did not come anymore, that I had to search for them. And that, my friend, was the moment I gave up."

♠ America puzzled Offenbach. He loved the gadgetry and the luxuries. The advertising fascinated him. He loved American women for their beauty and grace. But he disdained the standard money set in the American society. "Offenbach must be a great musician," he once overheard. "He gets a thousand dollars an evening for just conducting."

♠ Schumann and Liszt had an outspoken relationship. Although Schumann was inspired by Liszt's playing, he was less impressed with Liszt's flash and theatricality. He once said to Clara, "Art, as we know it – you when you play, I when I compose – art has an intimacy and charm that is worth more to me than all of Liszt's splendid tinsel."

♠ Fighting a writer's block, Franz Von Suppe once wrote a cookbook before he could return to writing his operettas. *Go figure.*

♠ Rossini and friends were talking about life and art. "My immortality?" declared Rossini. "Do you know what will survive me? The third act of *Tell*, the second act of *Otello*, and *The Barber of Seville* from one end to the other."

The trouble with schmucks

Schmucks feed on society like locust. I worked with a deejay whose signature hygiene cost me a fortune in disinfectants. Another became a nuisance trying to convert me into an *evangelical* Christian. A wealthy guy who failed to get a gig on the station where I worked bought it so that he could. Looking back, some of my radio employers were the biggest schmucks you could imagine. For them, I could have played a concerto for five kazoo and six saucepans and it would have made little difference as long as it made big bucks. Some had the morals and humanity of Caligula. Twice at WFMR, a classical station in Milwaukee, I was fired on my way out the door on a Friday after finishing my show. I knew of a deejay at another radio station who was fired in his hospital bed. Another returned to work after vacation only to find someone else working in his spot. But then, schmucks lurk in every corner of the world, don't they?

♠ In 1940, the Soviets passed a law requiring all employees to work eight-hour days. It became a bureaucratic nightmare. One opera manager went so far as prohibiting a performance of Tchaikovsky's *Eugene Onegin* because one character would have been killed at the end of the second act and, thereby, not worked his full eight hours. So everything was held up. Finally, after much discussion, permission was granted on the condition that the actor should remain backstage in costume and makeup till the end of the opera.

♠ Bach was court composer and choirmaster at Weimar when offered a gig at the court in Cothen. Wilhelm Ernst, unwilling to lose his famous musician to a better job with better pay, threw Bach in prison for a month. Bach was finally released on December 2, 1717, given an unfavorable discharge and sent on his way. As a final blow, the Weimar court tampered with official records to erase any memory of Bach – *Who?*

♠ Johann Strauss Jr. began composing waltzes at age six. Even back then, Johann Strauss Sr. didn't like the competition, so for years he told his son to find something else to do in life, like banking. He once locked up his son's violin, but Strauss' mother had a key and helped little Strauss practice.

♠ In 1844, the 19-year-old Johann Strauss Jr. made his debut as leader of his own orchestra. So jealous was Strauss Sr. that he tried everything to stop the concert. Nothing worked. Then Strauss Sr. sent a pack of his friends to disrupt the evening. They booed and cackled, but people hushed them up. The night was such a smashing hit that Strauss Jr. played his closing number 19 times for encore. At the end he played one of his father's waltzes, which mellowed the rowdy bunch.

♠ Samuel Goldwyn, the Hollywood mogul, was negotiating with Jascha Heifetz for a screen appearance. Heifetz mentioned his price and Goldwyn said it was too high. "Money isn't everything, Mr. Heifetz," said Goldwin. "I can make you famous."

♠ Mozart hated the Archbishop of Salzburg, Colleredo, for a number reasons. One went back to the time Mozart was 12 years old and Colleredo had commissioned him to write an opera. Fearing someone might help Mozart with the composition, the archbishop had him locked up in a little room for a week. Mozart did write the opera – *La Finta Semplice.*

♠ In Hollywood, Stravinsky surprised a producer by demanding $2,000 a week to write a movie score. "Why, for that kind of money I can get Al Newman," said the producer, meaning composer Alfred Newman.

♠ At one time Giuseppe Verdi had a clause in his contract with opera producers that fined them 1,000 francs every time they made cuts in his score. *Way to go, man.*

♠ Antonin Dvorak's publisher Fritz Simrock paid him 200 marks for the first set of the Slavonic Dances, the Op. 46. Simrock made a fortune on them. For the Op. 72 set, however, by which time Dvorak had become wise to the ways of the world, Simrock coughed up 3,000 marks. *Way to go, Anton.*

♠ A publisher paid Johann Strauss Jr. 15 pounds for The Blue Danube Waltz. *Thanks for nothing.*

♠ Liszt was court music director at Weimar, Germany, where music thrived under him. Liszt, known for his lavish tastes, was living with his mistress Princess Carolyne Sayn-Wittgenstein. In 1885, his patron, the Grand Duke Charles Frederick, died and Grand Duke Alexander succeeded him. Liszt's fortunes changed, as the new duke was more interested in theatre. Also, by then people had had enough of Liszt's scandalous lifestyle. Liszt resigned on bad terms, complaining, "Counts welcome great men provided they cease to be great the moment they come to court."

♠ A court order in Vienna informed Mozart to submit his salary. Mozart wrote back: "Too much for what I have done. Too little for what I could have done."

♠ Rossini didn't want an overture for *The Thieving Magpie*. No way, said the theatre manager, give me my overture. So he locked up Rossini in the opera house attic with pen and paper – and four burly stagehands. Well, Rossini wrote the overture, throwing each finished page out the window to the copyist waiting below.

♠ Cherubini was walking in Paris when it started to rain. An acquaintance stopped and offered his carriage to the composer. Cherubini gladly accepted. The man then said, "Mister Cherubini, will you lend me your umbrella?" Cherubini shook his head. "No, I never lend my umbrella," he said, and drove off, leaving the man in pouring rain.

♠ Handel's father, a barber-surgeon, cared little for music and musicians. Handel's mother, who felt differently, snuck a clavichord into the attic so that the young boy could practice. When the court duke heard Handel play the organ, he ordered the father to provide the boy with music lessons.

♠ On their first Russian tour, Johann Strauss Jr. and his orchestra had barely crossed the Silesia frontier when the authorities took them for spies. After locking them up in a freezing warehouse, they were shipped out to General Abramovich, the Russian commandant of occupied Warsaw. Even the Austrian consul failed to gain their release. To prove his innocence, Strauss convinced Abramovich to allow a private concert for him at police headquarters. Even though Abramovich loved the show, he claimed they were fakes, and packed them in a crummy hotel in their underwear. Friends finally got to the czarina, who was visiting Laschenski Castle near Warsaw. She commanded a gala concert before her a week later. And it was a smash. Abramovich apologized to Strauss, claiming it was nothing personal. "It was either you or I," he said. "If you were a spy, I would have ended up in Siberia. So I felt I was better off throwing the whole orchestra out of the country." *It's hard to argue with a schmuck.*

What's in a name?

I was named Uballit (Obelit in the English spelling, for some reason) after the Assyrian King Ashur Uballit I (1354-1326 B.C.) in whose reign Assyria emerged as a powerful empire. My heritage is Assyrian. Since teachers at Senn High School in Chicago struggled with the pronunciation of my first name, they called me Obie. Through my radio years, I received letters addressed to Yobie, Oobie, Oboe, O.B., and Bob – go figure that one. In recent years I have started receiving junk mail addressed to Obelit L. Yadgar, and Obelit J. Yadgar. Folks, I do not have a middle name. Of course, not having a middle name, I also walked into a slapstick comedy my first day as a draftee in the U.S. Army:

"What's your middle name, soldier?"

"I don't have a middle name, sergeant."

"What the hell you mean you don' have a middle name?"

"My parents didn't give one, sir."

"Don't call me sir."

"Yes, sir – yes, sergeant."

"What kind of parents don't give their kid a middle name?"

"My parents, sergeant."

"The hell is this? Everybody's got a middle name."

"Maybe they though my name already had balls, sergeant."

He writes down NMN. "Get your ass moving in line, soldier."

♠ I doubt Jacque Offenbach ever served in the army, but sometimes he would sign his name *O. de Cologne.* You see, Offenbach's grandfather, Juda Eberst, a singer and music teacher, settled in

Offenbach-am-Main, a suburb of Frankfurt, Germany. His son Isaac Juda Eberst, also musical, left home at 20, wandering around Germany, before settling down in Duetz. When people started calling him *Der Offenbacher*, he liked the reference and changed his name to Offenbach. In 1816, Isaac relocated his family to Cologne. His seventh child, Jakob, born on June 20, 1819, lived most of his composing life in Paris as Jacque Offenbach.

♠ Franz Von Suppe was known as the *German Offenbach* and the *Father of the Viennese Operetta.*

♠ In Paris, Rossini was known as *Monsieur Crescendo.*

♠ Robert Schumann had a lifelong affair with wordplay and anagrams. While in Mannheim on a break from law studies at the University of Heidelberg, he met a woman at a ball. Her name was Meta Abeg. He translated her name into musical notation by writing a variation on the notes A, Bb, E, G. The music is known the *Abeg Variations.*

♠ Clara Schumann was known as *Queen of the Piano.*

♠ In 1813, Rossini first wrote what was to become *The Barber of Seville* overture for *Aureliano in Palmyra*, an opera that is lost. In 1815, he used the same overture for *Elizabeth, Queen of England*. Waiting until the last day to write the overture as usual, he just crossed out the old title and put the new one on the paper.

♠ Some of Schubert's friends called him *Chubby*, while others referred to him as *Little Mushroom.*

♠ *The Pigtail Organ* was a big hit at the Great Exhibition of 1851, in England, by connecting an organ keyboard to a system of pincers clamped onto the tails of pigs with squeals of a different pitch. Press the right keys and the pigs squealed out a suited melody. *While the audience loved the gizmo, I'm not sure if the pigs did.*

♠ Louis XIV, who danced in many productions in his court, once danced the role of the sun god, thereafter becoming known as the *Sun King.*

♠ Bach's father and uncle were identical twins whose wives couldn't tell them apart. The only way Bach's mother could distinguish between her husband Ambrosius and his brother was when the baby Bach said "Papa." *Hell, I'll believe anything.*

♠ *Seven Octaves* was the pseudonym Louis Moreau Gottschalk used to publish several works from 1859-1863, all dedicated "To my friend L.M. Gottschalk."

♠ Fingal's Cave is located on the island of Staffa in the Hebrides, about 50 miles off the Scottish coast. The 60-ft. cave opens in a great basalt arch into the sea. The legend of Fingal's Cave says that once upon a time a great castle belonging to King Fionn Na Ghal stood there. The name, from Gaelic, means "chief of valor." King Fionn Na Ghal ruled the kingdom of Morven. The third century warrior poet Ossian was his son. The cave inspired Mendelssohn's concert overture Fingal's Cave.

♠ Mozart rarely used Amadeus. He preferred the French version, *Amade*.

♠ Pyotr Tchaikovsky's mother, Alexandra Andreyevna Assier, who was of French descent, called her son *Pierre*.

♠ John Philip Sousa had a fear of recording, thinking it would hurt ticket sales to his band concerts. His players Arthur Pryor, Herbert L. Clark, Walter B. Rogers and Rosario Bourdon, therefore, fronted the band on many Sousa recordings.

♠ Although Tchaikovsky loved opera and found it irrepressible, he still called it a *false art*.

♠ Palestrina's name was Giovanni Pierluigi. He was born in Palestrina, a town near Rome, so he changed his name to Giovanni Pierluigi da Palestrina.

♠ Abbe Lorenzo da Ponte, who wrote the libretti for Mozart's operas *Cosi Fan Tutte*, *The Marriage of Figaro* and *Don Giovanni*, was kicked out of schools, jobs, and cities including Vienna. Eventually he came to New York and opened a grocery store. He was affectionately called *Lo Spiritoso Ignorante*. He ended his days teaching Italian at what later became Columbia University.

♠ E.T.A. Hoffmann wrote for a Leipzig newspaper under the name Johannes Kreisler. His stories were used for Offenbach's *Tales of Hoffman* and Tchaikovsky's *The Nutcracker*.

♠ *Mutual Insurance Company for the Defeat of Boredom* is how Offenbach referred to his Friday night parties in his Paris home. The guests, mostly writers and musicians, came in character costumes.

♠ Felix (as in Mendelssohn) in Latin means "happy" or "fortunate."

♠ Who was the greatest composer? Haydn and Beethoven nominated Handel. Berlioz called him a *tub of pork and beer*.

♠ According to his granddaughter, Sir Edward Elgar, who loved Bach, would play the Chromatic Fantasy and Fugue while waiting for his bath. Around the house the piece was known as the *Bath Tune*.

♠ *Le Beau Dussek* was how people referred to the Bohemian composer and piano virtuoso Jan Ladislav Dussek (1760-1812) for his glamorous and adventurous life that included many love affairs. Dussek was also the first virtuoso to place his piano sideways on stage so that people could see his handsome profile. Liszt often gets the credit for this touch of showbiz.

♠ *Salon composer par excellence* – Chopin's reputation in the 1830s Paris.

♠ Years ago it became fashionable to conduct without a score. The practice disturbed orchestra musicians, because they felt it distracted from the performance. Soon they began calling these conductors *Guess Conductors*.

♠ Thanks to his speed, by age 30 Rossini had written 23 operas, once five in a year. The aria "Die Tanti Palpiti," from *Tancredi*, became known as the *Rice Aria*, because he had dashed it off in the time it took to cook rice for his dinner.

♠ Eric Satie, called *The Velvet Gentleman*, sported a wild beard and a pince-nez. He wore gray velvet suits with high stiff collar and an immense cravat. He carried an umbrella, and some said he took his top hat to bed. Satie, who hated money, lived in a tiny room outside Paris and let no one in. After his death, friends found his room stocked to the ceiling with never-worn and moth-eaten gray velvet suits, shirts, waistcoats, and hundreds of high stiff collars.

♠ John Field, the Irish composer and virtuoso pianist who settled in St. Petersburg, Russia, gave rise to a school of piano playing that had such vigor and character that it prompted the city's nickname *Pianopolis*.

♠ Beethoven called Schubert *The Divine Spark.*

♠ The *Cossack Princess,* whose real name was Olga Janina, was obsessed with Liszt. Married at 15, she horsewhipped her husband and walked out on the second day. At 16 she was a mother. After being deported from Budapest, she fell for Liszt at a master class in Rome. Private classes followed. Liszt, having lived through a string of affairs, was cautious about new relationships, so he escaped to Villa d'Este in Tivoli outside Rome. Olga showed up one day disguised as a gardener's boy, planning on killing Liszt if he rejected her. By then, with Liszt isolated and lonely, they started a relationship. A new scandal followed. Worst, Olga had zero talent, and Liszt finally dumped her. Failing to kill him, and herself, she wrote some nasty things about Liszt in her memoirs – all 25 volumes. The *Cossack Princess* died in 1887.

♠ *Frederick the Great* (Frederick II of Prussia) had signed an edict forbidding coffee, claiming he and his ancestors were brought up on beer. Soldiers nourished on beer won the battles, he said, not those who drank coffee. Old Fred also wanted women to avoid drinking coffee, because he believed the brew made them sterile.

♣ In 1729, Vivaldi's brother Giuseppe, a hothead troublemaker, was put on trial. One witness said he didn't know Giuseppe's last name, but only that he was the brother of the "red-haired priest who plays the violin."

♠ The Leipzig Gewandhaus Orchestra, one of today's major orchestras, was founded in 1780. It played in the linen merchants market hall in Leipzig. Gewandhaus in German means "cloth hall" – thus Gewandhaus Orchestra or the "cloth hall" orchestra. Mendelssohn became its music director in October 1835.

♠ *Twenty-Four Violins* was the name of King Louis XIV's orchestra at his court in Versailles. After hearing Jean-Baptiste Lully play the violin in the court kitchen and promoting him to court music director, the king formed a special band for Lully named *Les Petites-Violins.*

♠ *Caffarelli* (Gaetano Majorano 1710-1783), *Farinelli* (Carlo Broschi 1705-1782), *Guadagni* (Gaetano Guadagni 1725-1792) and *Senesino* (Francesco Bernardi Senesino c.1685-c.1759) were superstar castrati who, like bullfighters, adapted single names. The superstar castrati were highly esteemed and well paid. Some women loved them despite the castrati's physical peculiarities (fat, bloated, coarse, effeminate, etc.). At one time 4,000 boys ages 7-9 were castrated in a year, but less than 1% became successful singers. The last castrato to perform on stage in England, in 1844, was one named *Pergetti*. Alessandro Moreschi, the last known castrato, died in Rome in 1922.

♠ *Panomonico* was the name Waetzel, a 19th century Austrian, gave to his musical invention built with a conglomeration of instruments to be played by one person. The *Panomonico* included 150 flageolets, 150 flutes, 50 oboes, 18 trumpets, 5 fanfares, 3 drums and 2 kettledrums, altogether 378 instruments. Archduke Charles of Austria purchased Waetzel's *Panomonico* to annoy noisy courtiers of his royal household.

♠ Rimsky-Korsakov's grandfather, a world-traveling admiral, tried to set himself apart from all the other Korsakovs in Russia by adding *Rimsky* to the family name. *Rimsky* means *Roman*. So the family became known as *Rimsky Korsakov*, or the *Roman Korsakov*.

♠ In 1935, British critic Neville Cardus, in the Manchester Guardian, referred to Rimsky-Korsakov as *a cultural aromatist*.

♠ Some accounts give Vivaldi's father as a baker and some a barber. He was also a violinist in the San Marco Orchestra. His red hair prompted his nickname of *Rossi*. His son, Antonio, an ordained priest as well as composer, would be known, because of his own red hair, as the *Red Priest*.

♠ Rossini retired from writing operas at age 37, though not altogether from composing. After *William Tell*, his last opera, he wrote a collection of piano pieces and songs under the title of *Sins of My Old Age*. Some of the pieces in the collection have colorful titles: "*Miscarriage of a Polish Mazurka*," "*Profound Sleep With Startled Awakening*," and "*Hygienic Prelude for Morning Use*."

♠ Wagner loved Johann Strauss' music. He called him *a magic fiddler* and a *demon of the Viennese popular spirit.*

♠ *Eusebius* and *Florestan* were Robert Schumann's pen names: *Eusebius* described his tender and dreamy self, and *Florestan*, his impetuous self.

♠ John Philip Sousa's Portuguese immigrant parents were so overwhelmed by the United States that they added the letters "USA" to their last name, which was SO. Hence the family became known as SOUSA.

♠ *La Gioconda,* the 1876 opera by Amilcare Ponchielli, is the same title Leonardo da Vinci gave to his painting the *Mona Lisa,* a term meaning "the smiling woman."

♠ The third in Handel's stable of troublesome prima donnas was Anna Maria del Po. She was so nasty and difficult that Handel nicknamed her *The Pig.*

♠ Tchaikovsky's family had an *Orchestrion,* a mechanical organ popular at the time, which was controlled by a wood cylinder and could play elaborate pieces by imitating orchestral effects.

♠ *Sunday Composer* is how Alexander Borodin referred to himself.

♠ *Le Six* (Le Seece) was a group of French composers comprised of Auric, Durey, Honneger, Milhaud, Poulenc, and Tailleferre. In 1920, Henri Collet gave the group its name. *Le Six* were influenced by Eric Satie's emphasis on simplicity as well as by the artistic ideals of Jean Cocteau. The name was in imitation of the *Moguchaya Kuchka,* a group of Russian Nationalistic Composers. *Moguchaya Kuchka,* or the *Mighty Five,* was comprised of Balakirev, Cui, Borodin, Rimsky-Korsakov and Mussorgsky.

♠ Chopin, a child prodigy in Warsaw, was referred to as *The second Mozart.*

♠ Tchaikovsky had a diverse view on composers. He was in awe of Beethoven, while he found Bach entertaining. He found Gluck attractive, and Handel fourth rate He liked some things by Haydn. He loved Bizet, Gounod and Delibes. Not so Berlioz.

Most of all, he loved Mozart. For him, no one was like Mozart. He called him *The Christ of Music* and said he was "the greatest of all the composers."

♠ Joseph Lanner was known as the *Mozart of Dance Music*. *Die Schonbrunner*, a waltz composed in 1842, was his swan song, when his orchestra played it 21 times that night at Dommayr's Café in Vienna. In the end, Lanner put down his violin and walked away from the stage. That was the last time on the stage as leader of his orchestra.

Forget the damn watch — Give me the money!

*A*lthough gifts delight the heart and lift the spirit, sometimes what will do the job far better is plain old cash. Forget the damn necktie; give me the money! I don't know when the world will realize that the artist will take the cash anytime.

♠ A lot of people gave the oft-broke Mozart gifts instead of cash. In 1777, he complained that with five gold watches, he planned to have watch pockets sewn on his trousers so that people could see he didn't need another watch.

♠ When Rossini was 70, friends and admirers said they had raised 20,000 francs to erect a monument in his honor. Although flattered by the thought, Rossini, who needed money, said, "Give me the twenty thousand and I'll stand on the pedestal."

♠ Feodor Chaliapin, on tour, had a free evening and spent it with a young woman. In the morning, he told her he would give her tickets for that evening's opera. The woman protested that tickets would do little to help her hunger. "When you're poor, you want bread," she declared. "If you wanted bread," Chaliapin said, "you should have spent the night with a baker."

♠At 18, broke and jobless, Haydn tried to get a job singing at the Shrine of the Virgin of Mariazell in Styria to no avail. Then he did the next best thing and sneaked into the choir, impressing them enough that they kept him on for a week. That week he had his first proper meal in months. They also took up a small collection to send him on his way back to Vienna, happy.

♠ A panhandler in Vienna, begging Mozart for money, went so far as claiming they were distant cousins. Mozart, broke at the time, took the beggar to a café and within a few minutes composed a minuet and a trio. He told the beggar to take it to a publisher – and keep the money from the sale.

♠ In 1792, Haydn received an honorary doctorate from Oxford University. For the occasion, he had submitted his Symphony No. 92, now known as the *Oxford* Symphony. Haydn, however, complained that the event had cost him considerable amount of money. He couldn't understand why he had to pay 1.5 guineas for the ringing of the bell at the ceremony. Transportation had cost him 6 guineas. Robe and cap had cost half a guinea to rent.

♠ Liszt used his wealth to help people whenever possible. When the city of Bonn was working on a statue of Beethoven and ran out of money, Liszt paid for it.

♠ Paderewski had red-gold hair, which fascinated the ladies. Everybody kept asking for a lock of this hair. Not to discourage the boss's appeal to female fans, Paderewski's secretary bought a dog with the same color hair to oblige them. There is a similar story about Johann Strauss Jr.

♠ Bach's salary as organist at the court in Mulhausen was the equivalent of $50 a year. The fringe benefits included 3 lbs. of fish, 2 cords of wood and 54 bushels of corn.

♠ Elgar and a friend were strolling to the concert hall when they heard a street musician give a fairly good rendition of Elgar's miniature Salute d'Amour. Elgar asked the fiddler if he had any idea what he was playing. "Yes, Salute d'Amour, by Sir Edward Elgar," said the fiddler. Elgar gave him a half a crown and said, "Take this. It's more than Elgar ever made out of it."

♠ The court of Frederick II (*The Great*) of Prussia (1712-1786) resonated with music. Himself a fine flutist and composer, the king packed his court with prominent musicians: the flutist-composer Johann Joachim Quantz; the brothers CH and JG Graun; the brothers Franz and Johann Benda; and Carl Philip Emanuel Bach.

The budget for 1744-45 listed their salaries as follows: CPE Bach, 300 thalers; CH Graun, 2,000 thalers; JG Graun, 1,200 thalers; Quantz, 2,000 thalers; and the Benda brothers, 800 thalers each. In the same season, the leading castrato was paid 3,000 thalers. CPE Bach complained about his salary until the king raised it to 800 thalers. CPE Bach also wrote his father JS Bach that the question had come up as to who was the most feared animal in the Prussian monarchy. "It is Madame Quantz's lap-dog," he wrote. "He is so terrifying that Madame Quantz quails before him. Herr Quantz, in turn, is afraid of Madame Quantz. And the greatest of all monarchs fears Herr Quantz."

♠ When Jenny Lind, the *Swedish Nightingale*, toured the U.S. in 1850 for P.T. Barnum, she earned $176,000.

♠ Josquin des Pres, the Flemish court composer to King Louis XII, did not receive the raise in salary old Louis had promised him. *Monsieur* Josquin des Pres, the smart man that he was, composed a motet on a phrase from the 119th Psalm: "Oh, think upon Thy servant as concerning Thy word." The king got the message, and gave him the raise. In appreciation, the composer wrote another motet from the same psalm: "Oh, Lord, Thou has dealt graciously with Thy servant." *Hallelujah!*

♠ As a gentleman, Fryderyk Chopin preferred not to dirty his hands with business matters. So he required his students to put his piano teaching fee on the mantle while he, Chopin, stood looking out the window.

♠ Count Johann George Von Braun-Camus, a Russian nobleman, presented Beethoven with a fine horse as a token of appreciation for Variations on a Russian Dance, which Beethoven dedicated to the baron's wife, Countess Anna Margarette. Beethoven rode the horse a few times and then forgot about the beast. Beethoven's servant, well aware of his master's forgetfulness, started his own rent-a-horse business, keeping all the money for himself. It was only when he gave Beethoven the bills for the horse's upkeep that Beethoven remembered the horse.

♠ By the mid-1780s, Haydn's reputation as a great composer had reached all over Europe and America. The Canon of Cadiz Cathedral in Spain asked him to compose instrumental music for the *Seven Last Words of Our Savior From the Cross*, which was music intended for Good Friday. For payment, Spain sent Haydn a large chocolate cake filled with gold coins.

♠ After seeing Dance of the Seven Veils in the opera *Salome*, Kaiser Wilhelm complained to Richard Strauss that *Salome* was scandalous and not expressive of proper German virtues. Replied Strauss, "That scandalous work bought me a villa at Garmisch."

♠ Rossini received many awards from the nobility. In Paris, King Charles named him Inspector General of Singing in France. Not that anyone could figure out what the title meant. Rossini, having been given a big salary and thinking that at least he should do something to earn it, took to wandering Paris and inspecting the songs of the street beggars and drunks.

♠ Johann Strauss Jr. came to the U.S. for the 1872 Boston Peace Jubilee and everyone wanted a lock of his hair – a popular custom at the time. Strauss' servant, who was a hustler, told the fans he would oblige them for a price. The only thing is that he made a wad of money by sending the suckers locks of hair from Strauss' dog.

♠ A young and poor actor got a part in Offenbach's operetta *Les Deux Aveugles* for a few francs a month. At the first rehearsal Offenbach told him to cross the stage and throw a sou into a blind man's hat. "I'm sorry, I can't take this role," begged the singer. "Why, isn't it important enough?" asked Offenbach. "No, sir, it's because of the sou," said the actor. "You see I haven't got one." So Offenbach raised his salary.

♠ In 1885, Tchaikovsky bought a small home in Klin, a charming little town about 50 miles northwest of Moscow. On his daily walks he had a habit of giving money to the town children who happened to cross his path. When news about the money spread, more kids kept showing up. Soon the village elders just happened to show up along his route.

♠ Arturo Toscanini was proud of the fine gold watch presented to him by the orchestra. During a particularly bad rehearsal, however, the angry Toscanini threw the watch to the floor and smashed it to bits with his foot. The players, shocked to see their fancy watch under Toscanini's raging heel, proceeded to play the best they could, with every note perfect. Only they didn't know that Toscanini had smashed a cheap watch he picked up from the local drugstore.

♠ Beethoven presented his Ninth Symphony to King Frederick Wilhelm III of Prussia. The king sent him a letter of appreciation and a diamond ring. Beethoven, who had no use for jewelry and needed money, tried pawning it, but, after examining the ring, the pawnbroker gave it back to him. The ring was a fake.

♠ The ruling family at the Lippe-Detmold court near Hanover, where Brahms had worked as music director, sent him as a Christmas gift the first six volumes of the definitive Bach. Brahms later discovered that the other volumes had been ordered in his name and that he had to pay for them. He told Clara Schumann about it. She told him that she had played three extra concerts there, but that instead of paying her in cash, they sent her a fake bracelet that was also hideous.

♠ In 1892, Antonin Dvorak came to America as head of the National Conservatory of Music in New York for the whopping annual salary of $15,000, at the time equivalent to 30,000 gulden in Czech currency. His salary at the Prague Conservatory had been 1,200 gulden. Plus, the New York gig included four months of vacation.

Oh, Shit!

Or when things go awry

Sometimes during a live show everything that can possibly go wrong ultimately does. No show is immune to disaster. It is during such times that the best you can do is to throw up your hands and quietly shout, "Oh, shit!" I am inclined to think many composers and performing companies have used the "S" word during production disasters.

♠ Disaster rained on one of the earliest productions of Gounod's opera *Faust*. Following the overture, only the left side of curtain went up, leaving half the stage hidden. This included Faust, who was looking into his crystal ball and singing *"Rien, je ne vois rien"* (Nothing! I see nothing). Right then someone in the audience yelled, *"Moi non plus"* (Me neither). Then when Mephistopheles was supposed to appear in a puff of smoke, the trap door jammed and the basso staggered onto the stage with a nasty bump on his head. *I can only imagine what happened next.*

♠ The death scene in *La Traviata*, at the opera's premiere in Venice on March 16, 1853, gave the audience something to laugh about. After all, Signora Salvini-Donatelli, playing Violetta who is dying of tuberculosis, was one of the fattest women in town.

♠ In the opera *La Traviata*, Violetta uses a bell to ring for her maid. In one production, the prop department forgot to put the bell at the proper location on the stage. When Violetta reached for it, it was not there. So without losing a beat, she pretended to shake a bell, announcing, "Tinkle-tinkle."

♠ *The Barber of Seville* opened on February 20, 1816, to catcalls and boos from the audience thanks to a series of mishaps on the stage. A string from Count Almaviva's guitar broke. Basilio stumbled over a trap door and was forced to sing "La Calunnia" with a handkerchief held to his bleeding nose. A black cat then scampered onto the stage. Figaro chased it in one direction, Bartolo in another. Finally the kitty scooted up Rosina's skirt. Rosina squealed, and right then Rossini stood up in the audience and applauded.

♠ In 1900, a touring company in El Paso, Texas, performed *The Barber of Seville* with a few minor cuts. When word of the cuts got around, the audience felt cheated and a riot broke out. Matters got so far out of hand that gunmen almost killed the impresario. The sheriff showed up and calm was restored only after it was announced that admission would be refunded. *Only in Texas.*

♠ *Das Liebesverbot* (The Ban on Love), Wagner's second completed opera, opened and closed in one night due to a string of mishaps: The orchestra got lost in the score, and the singers were not ready, one so frazzled that he sang arias from another opera. To top it off, the prima donna's jealous husband stormed onto the stage and slugged the tenor. *Otherwise things were okay.*

♠ In one Madrid production of Wagner's *Gotterdammerung*, Siegfried was so lousy that when Hagen speared him, the audience burst into a spontaneous ovation.

The importance of being useless as a critic

I stood on the beach in San Francisco hypnotized by the moon as it slowly sank into the Pacific Ocean. A boy and a girl nearby, who were wrapped around each other like vines, stopped smooching long enough for the boy to point to the moon and declare, "Man, look at that big old hairy thing." I had never heard a magnificent moon described in such a way. Years later, after reading a particularly unfavorable – and ridiculous – concert review of Brahms' second piano concerto by a local critic who thought he was H.L. Mencken, I remembered that boy's description of the moon and wondered if he had grown up to be this newspaper music critic. Were we at the same concert? Since that concert, every time I read a music review, I find myself on the beach in San Francisco howling at the moon.

♠ "Never pay attention to what critics say," Sibelius advised a student. "Remember, a statue has never been set up in honor of a critic."

♠ In 1896, *The Item*, a New Orleans newspaper, had no available music critic to cover Paderewski's concert, so the boxing editor was sent instead. "In my opinion, he is the best two-handed piano fighter that ever wore hair," the man wrote. "If I were a piano, I wouldn't travel as Paderewski's sparring partner for two-thirds of the gross receipts."

♠ A Viennese music critic died without leaving money for his funeral. His friends, trying to raise funds for the funeral, asked a well-known composer for a contribution. "What's my share?" he asked. "Thirty kronen, maestro," they said. "Here's sixty kronen," he said. "Bury two critics."

♠ Eric Satie, who disliked critics, once said, "Last year, I gave several lectures on Intelligence and Musicality in Animals. Today I shall speak to you about Intelligence and Musicality in Critics. The subject is very similar."

♠ "The most useless occupation in the world" – Rossini talking about critics.

♠ George Bernard Shaw was a great critic, but Jascha Heifetz frustrated him by always playing perfectly. So Shaw once took a jab at Heifetz by urging him to play one wrong note per concert just to prove he was human.

♠ In the 1860s, one critic, after seeing Wagner's opera *Die Meistersinger*, wrote: "Of all the clumsy, lumbering, boggling, baboon-blooded stuff I ever saw on a human stage, of all the affected, sapless, soul-less, beginningless, endless, topless, bottomless, topsy-turviest doggerel of sound I ever endured the deadliness of, that eternity of nothing was the deadliest."

♠ The reviews of Berlioz's dramatic symphony *Romeo and Juliet* were mostly negative. One critic even called it "an ill-greased syringe." Berlioz returned the compliment by calling the guy a "toad, swollen with imbecility." *You tell 'em, man.*

♠ Critics hailed the Chorus of Shepherds by Pierre Ducre. Berlioz, who conducted the first performance, claimed he had discovered the work in a closet. Except that Berlioz had written the piece, crediting the imaginary Pierre Ducre just to fool the critics. Later he expanded the work into *L'Enfance du Christ*, which became one of his most famous works.

♠ Two critics were arguing about modern composers. "Stravinsky," said the first critic. "Stravinsky is no good. Why, the only decent music he ever wrote was Bolero." The second critic shook his head and said, "But, Mischa, Stravinsky didn't write Bolero. Ravel wrote it. "See," said the first critic. "Stravinsky didn't even write that."

♠ Mendelssohn was strongly against critics and music journalists. He was opposed to the idea of writing about music rather than writing music.

♠ Beethoven frustrated his critics, many of whom were puzzled by his genius, and his complexity. One such critic wrote: "It is undeniable that Herr Van Beethoven goes his own way, but what a bizarre and painful way it is."

♠ "Often a charming melody is caricatured in a refrain of extreme vulgarity," said a French critic writing about Jacques Offenbach. "Our unfortunate country will plunge into ruin if she does not quickly recover her good sense and her good taste by throwing out once and for all these impudent corroders of the theatre." *Oh, dear, dear.*

♠ Henriette Sontag received a bad review from the publication *The Musical Standard*. "We hang on every note Madame Sontag sings," wrote the critic. "This proves the lady's great power of execution."

♠ Aside from calling Beethoven's Ninth Symphony "pages of stupid and hopelessly vulgar music," Philip Hale of the Boston Musical also wrote in his review on June 1, 1889: "Do you believe way down in the bottom of your heart that if this music had been written by Mr. John L. Tarbox, now living in Sandown, NH, any conductor here or in Europe could be persuaded to put it into rehearsal?"

♠ "The critics never change," said the 76-year-old violinist Mischa Elman. "I'm still getting the same notice I used to get as a child. They tell me I play very well for my age."

♠ Verdi was finishing *Il Trovatore* when an influential critic stopped by to hear some of the tunes from the opera. "Garbage! Rubbish! No good!" declared the critic afterward. "Thank you, my friend," Verdi said, undisturbed. "I'm writing a popular opera. If I had pleased you, I should have pleased no one else. I'm most grateful for your opinion."

♠ In the love scene from the opera *Zaza*, by Leoncavallo, Geraldine Farrar was baffled when her lover, Martinelli, sat on the sofa rather than take her in his arms. She leaned on the back of the sofa and whispered, "Are you ill?" The tenor replied, "No, my suspenders let go." Farrar tried to save the scene by being flirtatious on the back of the couch. The critics, alas, accused her of hogging the scene, which belongs to the tenor.

Then again, even critics deserve mercy:

♠ In 1836, Chopin gave a concert in Rouven, France, and received rave reviews from critic Ernest Legouve. Looking back at the contest held the previous year between Franz Liszt and Sigismond Thalberg, both piano giants, Legouve added, "In the future when the question is asked who is the greatest pianist in Europe, Liszt or Thalberg? Let the world reply, 'It's Chopin.'"

♠ Brahms was often compared to Beethoven. When his first symphony premiered in Vienna, the audience heard similarities with Beethoven's Ninth. "Any donkey can see that," offered Brahms. Brahms' friend, the critic Edward Hanslick, liked the symphony. He said, "No other composer has come as close to Beethoven's splendid work." People then started referring to Brahms' First as Beethoven's Tenth.

Musical quotations for every occasion

Almost

*O*h, how I envy people who can remember tons of quotes and zap you with them at just the right moment. My mind, I fear, cannot hold too many quotes. For that reason, early on in my radio career I started collecting all kinds of quotes. The ones here, listed in no particular order, are from the world of classical music – for almost every occasion.

♠ "The violin's a great instrument – too bad it's wasted on classical music" – I overheard one teenage punk rocker say this to his friend as they reflected on Itzhak Perlman's poster on the kiosk outside the Marcus Center for the Performing Arts, in Milwaukee, Wisconsin.

♠ "Music is the vapor of art. It is to poetry what reverie is to thought, what fluid is to liquid, what the ocean of clouds is to the ocean of waves" – Victor Hugo

♠ "Beethoven's music is music about music" – Friedrich Nietzsche.

♠ "Mozart's the boy for you – the broom that sweeps the cobwebs away" – Madge Wood (Barbara Bel Geddes) suggesting Mozart to Scottie Ferguson (James Stewart) after his mental breakdown, in Alfred Hitchcock's *Vertigo.*

♠ "An instrument to tickle human ears by friction of a horse's tail on the entrails of a cat"— Ambrose Bierce's description of the violin.

♠ "No one ever asks if you have heard Paganini, but if you have seen him" – Paganini.

♠ Hans Von Bulow (1830-1894), the renowned pianist, conductor and composer, is credited with coining the phrase "The Three B's" of classical music – Bach, Beethoven and Brahms. In 1880, he wrote in a young lady's notebook: "I believe in Bach, the Father; Beethoven, the Son; and Brahms, the Holy Ghost of Music."

♠ "The best ideas come to me when I polish my shoes in the morning" – Brahms.

♠ "We are very lucky that Paganini did not write an opera, otherwise it would be terrible for us" – Rossini.

♠ "There is a fine line between genius and insanity," said Oscar Levant. "I have erased this line."

♠ "If I don't practice for one day, I know it," said Ignacy Paderewski. "If I don't practice for two days, the critics know it. If I don't practice for three days, the audience knows it."

♠ "A fugue is a piece of music in which the voices come in one by one, and the audience goes out one by one."

♠ "Music is not illusion, but revelation" – Tchaikovsky.

♠ "There is music in the air, music all around us. The world is full of it, and you simply take as much as you require" – Sir Edward Elgar.

♠ "Music is the only noise for which one is obliged to pay" – Alexandre Dumas.

♠ "I have more taste than previously, but no longer any genius" – Jean Philip Rameau near the end of his life.

♠ "Saint-Saens knows everything but lacks inexperience" – Berlioz.

♠ "A true music lover is one who on hearing a blond soprano singing in the bathtub puts his ear to the keyhole."

♠ "The nations would compete to posses such a jewel within their fortified walls" – Haydn reflecting on his dear friend Mozart.

♠ "Where the speech of man stops short, then the art of music begins" – Wagner.

♠ "This one's learned it from God" – Schubert's piano and organ teacher, Wenzel Ruzicka, at the Imperial Royal Seminary in Vienna.

♠ "I have one terrible, invincible vice, that of working all the time," declared Offenbach. "I'm sorry for those people who do not like my music, for I shall certainly die with a tune on the tip of my pen."

♠ "Everything beautiful is difficult, the short the most difficult" – Schumann.

♠ "The esthetic experience is the same in any art; only the materials differ" – Schumann.

♠ Mendelssohn grandfather was the famous Jewish philosopher Moses Mendelssohn. Mendelssohn's father, Abraham, was a successful Berlin banker. Abraham, for all his success, didn't have the star power his father and son had. He once said in frustration: "When I was young, I was the son of Moses Mendelssohn. Now I am the father of Felix Mendelssohn. What am I really, just a dash between two generations?" He also used to say: "Formerly I was the son of my father. Now I am the father of my son."

♠ "I don't know how, with no vibrato, Bach could have so many sons" – Paul Hindemith.

♠ George Bernard Shaw said that the bass arias of Sarastro in Mozart's *The Magic Flute* were the only music that would not sound out of place in the mouth of God.

♠ "This boy will cause us all to be forgotten" – composer Johann Adolph Hasse, after hearing the young Mozart at the keyboard.

♠ Gounod loved Mozart. He said: "When I was twenty, I just said, 'I.' At thirty I said, 'I and Mozart.' At forty, 'Mozart and I.' And now, at sixty, I say quietly and modestly, 'Mozart.'"

♠ "When I first came here, I found among the English many good players and no composers, but now they are all composers and no players" – Handel in England.

♠ "My grandfather used to say to talk well and eloquently is a great art, but that an equally great one is to know the right moment to stop" – Mozart.

♠ "Beethoven I take twice a week, Haydn four times, and Mozart everyday" – Rossini, when asked about his favorite composer among the greats.

♠ "To be natural is greater than to be original" – Rossini.

♠ "Give me a laundry list and I'll set it to music" – Rossini.

♠ "I admire and love Mozart," said Schopenhauer, "and go to all concerts where Beethoven symphonies are played, but when one has heard much Rossini, everything else is ponderous contrast."

♠ "Mozart is happiness before it has gotten defined" – Arthur Miller.

♠ Paris in the 1820s and the 1830s, where both Liszt and Chopin lived (Chopin from the 30s), was a sinful and colorful city. The German poet Heinrich Heine wrote about it: "When dear God is bored in heaven, he opens the window and contemplates the boulevards of Paris."

♠ "I am happier when I have something to compose, for that, after all, is my sole delight and passion" – Mozart.

♠ "Music must never offend the ear. It must please the hearer. In other words, it must never cease to be music" – Mozart.

♠ "One should take a spoonful of music a day" – Moritz von Schwind, the German painter and Schubert's friend, who drew many pictures of Schubert.

♠ "It may be a good thing to copy reality, but to invent reality is much better" – Verdi.

♠ Tennyson described Mendelssohn's as "the most perfect face I have ever seen."

♠ "Music in its flexibility offers inexhaustible resources," said Saint-Saens. "Give Mozart a fairy tale, and he creates without effort an immortal masterpiece."

♠ "Before I had my beard, I looked like Clara Schumann's son, and now with it, I look like her father" – Brahms.

♠ "Musical ideas sprang to my mind like a flight of butterflies, and all I had to do was to stretch out my hand to catch them"— Charles Gounod recalling life in Provence.

♠ "If God chose to speak to man, he would employ the music of Haydn, but if he desired to hear an earthly musician, he would select Boccherini" – a contemporary.

♠ "I believe music to be the ideal language of the soul," reflected Robert Schumann. "Some think it is only intended to tickle the ear, while others treat it like a mathematical calculation."

♠ For a long time rumor was that Franz Xaver Sussmayer had composed Mozart's *Requiem*. When Beethoven was asked about it, he replied, "If Mozart did not compose it, then the man who did compose it was a Mozart."

♠ "A tune for Schubert was the most natural way of releasing emotion."

♠ Mendelssohn, who met Chopin in Paris, engaged him as guest soloist with the Gewandhaus Orchestra. They also performed their own music together in private. Their relationship was uneasy, however, for neither understood the other. Talking about their playing, Mendelssohn said they were "as if a Cherokee and a Kaffir had met for a chat."

♠ "Next to God, it is Shakespeare who has created most," said Berlioz. "To have reached the age of forty-five or fifty and not known Hamlet, it's like having spent all of one's years in a coal mine."

♠ "It sometimes seems to me as if I did not belong to this world at all" – Schubert.

♠ "A conductor's real task is to make himself ostensibly almost superfluous," said Liszt. "We are pilots, not workers."

♠ "My name is Solomon, and I have come from London to fetch you" – concert promoter Johann Peter Solomon at Haydn's door in Vienna, in December 1790.

♠ "I shall be sorry when I come back to Vienna to feel the loss of Mozart," said Haydn in London after hearing of Mozart's death. "More than a century will pass before a talent such as his will be found again."

♠ "Go, you are the fortunate one, for you will give joy and happiness to many people. There is nothing finer" – Beethoven, kissing Liszt's forehead after young Liszt's concert debut in Vienna, in 1822, where Liszt played the opening movement of Beethoven's Piano Concerto in C.

♠ "Respectable people don't write music, or make love, as a career" – Alexander Borodin.

♠ "Works of art are not created; they are there, waiting to be discovered" – Elgar.

♠ "I am going too fast too soon," uttered Ferdinand Herold on his deathbed. "I was just beginning to understand the stage."

♠ "Together with the puzzle, he gives you the solution" – composer and virtuoso pianist Ferrucio Busoni talking about Mozart.

♠ In April 1845 in Paris, after hearing the young Louis Moreau Gottschalk play the E-Minor Piano Concerto at a private concert, Chopin congratulated him, saying, "Give me your hand, my child. I predict that you will become the king of pianists."

♠ "Art and life are not two different things" – Mendelssohn.

♠ "If Paganini is perfection, then Kalkbrenner is at least his equal, but in a completely different way" – Chopin speaking in Paris about his friend, the pianist and composer Friedrich Kalkbrenner.

♠ "Mozart is sunshine" – Dvorak.

♠ "Without craftsmanship inspiration is a mere reed shaken in the wind" – Brahms.

♠ "Beethoven's music parallels the pillar of smoke and fire which led the Israelites through the desert, a pillar of smoke to lead us by day, and a pillar of fire to light the night" – Franz Liszt, 1852.

♠ "Every theatre is a lunatic asylum," somebody once said, "but opera is the ward for incurable."

♠ When asked which of his operas he thought best, Gaetano Donizetti replied, "How can I say which? A father always has a preference for a crippled child, and I have so many."

♠ "Oh, God, how much is still to be in this splendid art, even by such a man as I have been" – Haydn in a letter in 1799 to George August Griesinger.

♠ "I wanted to become a Mozart in composition and a Liszt in technique" – Bedrich Smetana.

♠ Brahms began growing his great beard in his 40s. When a friend asked him about it, Brahms said, "A clean-shaven man is taken for an actor or a priest."

♠ "That boy doesn't sing; he crows" – Empress Maria Theresa's comment in November 1749, when Haydn's voice broke and he was fired from the chorus at Vienna's St. Stephens Cathedral.

♠ Gottschalk was the first American pianist of international fame. He said graciously, "I was the first American pianist, not in stature, but in time."

♠ "You cannot imagine how it spoils one to have been a child prodigy" – Liszt.

♠ "There is a master of the orchestra, so great a master that one never fails to hear a single note of any instrument" – Brahms on Strauss.

♠ "Johann Strauss, the Waltz King, personally, is evidently a good fellow," wrote the *New York World* in 1872. "He talks only German, but smiles in all languages."

♠ "Friends often flatter me that I have some genius, but Mozart stood far above me" – Haydn speaking of his dear friend.

♠ "The state should keep me," said Franz Schubert. "I have come into the world for no other purpose but to compose."

♠ "A landscape, torn by mists and clouds, in which I can see ruins of old churches, as well as of Greek temples – that is Brahms" – Edvard Grieg.

♠ "You make upon me the impression of a man who has several heads, several hearts and several souls" – Haydn to Beethoven.

♠ "Opera is a bizarre mixture of poetry and music where the writer and the composer, equally embarrassed by each other, go to a lot of trouble to create an abomination" – Charles de Saint-Evremont.

♠ "Opera is an exotic and irrational entertainment" – Dr. Samuel Johnson.

♠ "Opera is when a guy gets stabbed in the back and instead of bleeding, he sings" – Ed Gardner.

♠ "Opera in English is like baseball in Italian."

♠ "Sleep is an excellent way of listening to an opera" – James Stephens.

♠ "I seem to write an opera about every 20 years," said Virgil Thomson. "If you live long enough, you can write four operas."

♠ "I am sure my music has a taste of codfish in it" – Edvard Grieg.

♠ "It is his voice that remains one of the most majestic ever lifted in praise of love, of beauty, and of the art of music" – somebody said that of Handel.

♠ "You should not perspire when conducting; only the audience should get warm" – Richard Strauss.

♠ "Where Mozart is, Haydn cannot appear" – Haydn turning down the invitation to attend the coronation of Emperor Leopold II in Prague.

♠ "Should I have to spend my money in order to be like those idiots? Never in this world" – Handel balking at the expenses he would incur if he accepted an honorary degree from Oxford.

♠ "If I weren't reasonably placid," said Joan Sutherland, "I don't think I could cope with this life. To be a diva, you've got to be like a horse."

♠ "Nobody really sings in an opera," said Amelita Galli-Curci. "They just make loud noises."

♠ "I will not be sued," said Maria Callas. "I have the voice of an angel."

♠ "A librettist is a mere drudge in the world of opera" – Robertson Davies.

♠ "Speech is silver, but silence, silence at the right time, is pure gold" – one of Beethoven's favorite proverbs, which he also set to music.

♠ "Listen to music religiously as if it were the last strain you might hear" – Henry David Thoreau.

♠ "Music is well said to be the speech of angels" – Thomas Carlyle.

♠ "Bach is a sign of God, clear, yet inexplicable" – Carl Friedrich Zelter.

♠ "Art demands of us that we shall not stand still" – Beethoven.

♠ "I only know two tunes; one is 'Yankee Doodle' and the other isn't" – U.S. Grant.

♠ "Bach heals and pacifies all men and all things" – Sir Edward Elgar.

♠ "Music is the most sensuous of arts to loving souls" – Honore Balzac.

♠ "In truth, there is nothing like music to fill the moment with substance, whether it attune the quiet mind to reverence and worship, or whether it make the mobile senses dance in exultation" – Goethe, 1829.

♠ In 1826, Beethoven caught a cold, which turned into pneumonia, and he died three months later, in 1827. On his deathbed he is reputed to have raised a fist and declared, "The comedy is ended."

♠ "Music excavates Heaven" – Charles Baudelaire.

♠ "Music is love in search of a word" – Sidney Lanier.

♠ "Music is the best means we have of digesting time" – W.H. Auden.

♠ "Without music life would be a mistake" – Friedrich Nietzsche.

♠ "If the king loves music, there is little wrong in the land" – Meng-Tzu, the Chinese philosopher who flourished around 289 B.C.

♠ "Those who understand my music must be freed by it from all the miseries that others drag about within themselves" – Beethoven.

♠ "Usually I have to wait for other people to tell me when I have new ideas, because I never know this myself" – Beethoven.

♠ "Bach is the prince of clavier and organ players" – George Andreas Sorge.

♠ "God is God and Bach is Bach" – Hector Berlioz.

♠ The difference between a good and a bad conductor is that one has the score in his head, and the other has his head in the score" – F.H. Cowen.

♠ "To be a composer and not a musician is a tragedy; it is to have genius and not talent" – Nadia Boulanger.

♠ This is how Ambrose Bierce described noise: "A stench in the ear. Undomesticated music. The chief product and authenticating sign of civilization."

♠ "Hell is full of musical amateurs, music is the brandy of the damned" – George Bernard Shaw.

♠ One yearns unspeakably for a composer who gives out his pair of honest themes, and then develops them with both ears open, and then recapitulates them unashamed, and hangs a coda to them, and then shuts up!" – H.L. Mencken.

♠ "A score should be in the conductor's head, not the conductor's head in the score" – Hans Von Bulow.

♠ "Without a song the bush knife is dull" – a West African proverb.

♠ "If music be the breakfast food of love, kindly do not disturb until lunchtime" – James Agee.

♠ "If a man lacks the virtues proper to humanity, what has he to do with music?" – Confucius.

♠ "And when love speaks, the voices of all the gods makes heaven drowsy with harmony" – Shakespeare.

♠ "Music is the melody whose text is the world" – Arthur Schopenhauer.

♠ "Music is a beautiful opiate, if you don't take it too seriously" – Henry Miller.

♠ "Most string quartets, as ensembles, have a basement and an attic, and the lift is not working" – Neville Cardus.

♠ "Music produces a kind of pleasure which human nature cannot do without" – Confucius.

♠ "When a musician has forgot his note, he makes as though a crumb stuck in his throat" – John Clark, 1639.

♠ "Why do these damn musicians make me say a thing twice when I said it only once?" – Tennyson on composers repeating the stanzas from his poems set to music.

♠ "Always ask for advice but never take it" – Gustav Holst.

♠ "The worse the time, the quicker the avalanche of ideas for composition" – Leos Janacek.

♠ "I am three times homeless: as a native of Bohemia in Austria, as an Austrian among Germans, and as a Jew throughout the world" – Gustav Mahler.

♠ "Meyerbeer had the luck to be talented, but above all, the talent to be lucky" – Berlioz.

♠ "I would rather die than be bored" – Goethe's words, Schubert's motto.

♠ "Pain sharpens the understanding and strengthens the mind, whereas joy seldom troubles about the former and softens the latter and makes it frivolous" – Schubert, 1824.

♠ "Above all, do not analyze my music – love it" – Francis Poulenc.

♠ "Music, when soft voices die, vibrates in the memory" – Shelly.

♠ "Music is a science that would have us laugh and sing and dance" – Guillaume de Machaut.

♠ "The other arts persuade us, but music takes us by surprise" – Eduard Hanslick.

♠ "It can be made anywhere, is invisible, and does not smell" – W.H. Auden on music.

♠ "Tis' a sure sign that work goes on merrily, when folks sing at it" – Isaac Bickerstaffe, 1765.

♠ "The song that we hear with our ears is only the song that is sung in our hearts" – Ouida, from *Ariodante.*

♠ "He who loves not wine, woman, and song remains a fool his whole life long" – Martin Luther.

♠ "You must hear the bird's song without attempting to render it into nouns and verbs" – Ralph Waldo Emerson.

"A novel is like a bow, and the violin that produces the sounds is the reader's soul" – Stendhal.

♠ "O Mozart, immortal Mozart, how many, how infinitely many inspiring suggestions of a finer, better life you have left in our soul" – from Schubert's diary.

♠ "And if there is music in heaven, where do the musicians go when they have to tune their instruments?"

♠ "Music expresses that which cannot be said and on which it is impossible to be silent" – Victor Hugo.

♠ "Music isn't a luxury. It's a habit, like smoking and spitting" – Percy Granger.

♠ "Music washes away from the soul the dust of everyday life."

♠ "Music is the only sensual pleasure without vice" – Dr. Samuel Johnson.

♠ "The business of music should in some measure lead to the love of the beautiful" – Plato.

♠ "The man who has music in his soul will be most in love with the loveliest"—Plato.

♠ "Even the beautiful must die, but it is glorious to be a song of lament in the mouth of a friend" – Schiller.

Appetite is for the stomach what love is for the heart

Rossini

"The art of dining well is no slight art, the pleasure not a slight pleasure," said the philosopher Montaigne. I believed that long before I had heard of Montaigne. Growing up poor made me grateful for what food I received, and every meal, therefore, no matter how slight, became a pleasure. Many of the great composers also loved food, so it's nice to feel a kinship with them.

♠ Brahms was ill and the doctor told him to go on a diet. "But how can I?" said Brahms. "I am invited to dine with Strauss, and we are going to have chicken with paprika." The doctor said, "That is out of the question. You cannot eat that." Brahms shrugged. "Very well then. Please consider that I did not come to consult you until tomorrow."

♠ One of Beethoven's favorite eats was a Zwieback cookie dunked in wine. He also loved macaroni and Parmesan cheese. As for his morning coffee, he is reputed to have ground 60 coffee beans.

♠ Rossini, who liked to snack on bologna sandwiches, had assigned the second oboe in the opera orchestra to make sandwiches for him during the first intermission. Since in a number of Rossini operas the oboe plays only in the beginning and in the ending, we can assume the middle was reserved for the oboist to make sandwiches.

♠ A starving musician looking for a handout called on Rossini, saying he would work for it. So he began playing the Prayer from Rossini's opera *Moses* on glasses of water. Halfway through the performance, Rossini's servant entered with an important message. "I'll be with you in a moment," Rossini told him. "This gentleman is ringing my Prayer."

♠ The 15-year-old Bach, who had walked 25 miles from Hamburg to Luneberg to hear organist Jan Reinken, was returning home when he sank on the ground outside a tavern window, hungry and exhausted, the smell of fish cooking making him weak. Soon two fish heads were tossed out the window. Bach caught them and began devouring his cache. He bit on something metallic in the first fish head. It was a coin. The second fish head contained a coin as well. Laughing with his good luck, he pocketed the money and marched back to Hamburg to hear Reinken again. Five years later Bach walked 200 miles to hear Dietrich Buxtehude play.

♠ Beethoven was known for being absent-minded. Dorothea Von Ertmann, a student at whose house Beethoven frequently dined, recalled that often he would complain he didn't have an appetite. She said it was because he had forgotten he had just put away a feast. Then again, sometimes he would forget to eat for long hours.

♠ "The stomach is the conductor, who rules the grand orchestra of our passion, and rouses it into action" – Rossini.

♠ Brahms was guest at a wine maker's home when the host uncorked a rare bottle of wine and announced, "What Brahms is among composers, this Rauthaler is among wines." Brahms responded, "In that case, let's drink a bottle of Bach."

♠ A hostess once said to Rossini, "Maestro, you have conferred a great honor upon us by accepting our invitation to dine. When will you come to dinner again?" Rossini licked his chops and said, "Right away, Madame."

♠ Rossini and Meyerbeer were friendly rivals. Someone once asked Rossini what he thought of Meyerbeer. "Meyerbeer and I are worlds apart," said Rossini. "He likes sauerkraut and I like macaroni."

♠ Georges-Auguste Escoffier (1846-1935), the renowned chef at London's Savoy Hotel, was desperate to attend a gala performance by Dame Nellie Melba (Helen Porter Mitchell), the famous Australian soprano. Finally Dame Nellie managed to get him a pair of tickets. The next day at lunch Escoffier had an extraordinary dessert for her, which he had named Peach Melba.

♠ In his later years in Vienna, Brahms usually ate in the back room of the Red Hedgehog. The café went out of its way to prepare his food, and always had a cask of Hungarian wine for his private delight.

♠ Baron James Rothschild sent Rossini some splendid grapes from his vineyard. Rossini wrote back and thanked him, adding, "Splendid though your grapes certainly are, I don't take my wine in pills." Baron Rothschild got the message and sent Rossini some of his celebrated wine.

♠ "I know of no more admirable occupation than eating, that is, really eating," said Rossini. "Appetite is for the stomach what love is for the heart."

♠ "Eating, loving, singing and digesting are, in truth, the four acts of the comic opera known as life," said Rossini, "and they pass like the bubbles of a bottle of champagne. Whoever lets them break without having enjoyed them is a complete fool."

♠ The English composer Thomas Arne was at an inn, hungry and broke. A leg of mutton cooked on the spit for a party of gentlemen. The resourceful Arne sneaked into the kitchen and sprinkled the mutton with pieces of cut violin string. Well, the gentlemen refused the meat, claiming it was full of maggots. "Here, give it to me," Arne stepped in. "Oh, sir, you can't eat it," warned the waiter. "Nay, never mind," said Arne. "Fiddlers have strong stomachs." He then set the food in front of him, scraped off the bits of violin string, and had himself a feast of mutton – on the gentlemen.

♠ Beethoven entered the Swan Tavern in Vienna for lunch one day deep in thought and immediately dropped in a chair and began writing in his sketchbook. The waiter, aware of Beethoven's peculiarities, left him alone. Half an hour later he checked on Beethoven and found him still working in his notebook, and left him alone. An hour passed when suddenly Beethoven's voice boomed, "My bill." Puzzled, the waiter said, "But, your honor, you haven't ordered anything yet." Beethoven gave him a stern look. "Haven't I? Well, then, hurry along, get something to eat – and leave me alone."

♠ Rossini cried only three times in his life: once at the premiere of *The Barber of Seville*, because it was a disaster; once when he heard a fellow composer sing; and once on a boat ride when the stuffed turkey dinner accidentally fell overboard.

♠ Offenbach often lunched at Peter's restaurant in Paris, topping it with cake, coffee and cigar. When a bear act was added, it irritated Offenbach so much that he stopped going there for his lunches. He returned only after they dumped the bear act.

Delicious curiosities and stuff

The head is the world's biggest attic for storing stuff. Never having been a time-and-temperature deejay, or one given to silly chatter just to say something, I always looked for tidbits from the world of classical music with which to pepper my conversation. The more the listeners liked the stuff, the more I packed in my head. As time went on, my list grew. Here is some of that *stuff.* I don't know what you're going to do with it, except maybe use it to drive away bores who corner you at parties.

♠ Antonio Stradivari labeled his first violin in 1666.

♠ Beethoven sometimes would lather his face and then forget to shave.

♠ Bayreuth produces only Wagner's operas.

♠ The Grand Duke Michael Pavlovich would discipline his officers by making them sit through all of Michael Glinka's opera *Russlan and Ludmila.*

♠ Mozart was a master of the *shtick.* People would sing and he would make sonatas out of the music. He would shoot pool with one hand and compose with the other. He would cover the piano keyboard with a napkin and play – perfectly.

♠ Offenbach, who loved American women, had a theory about why they carried purses. He said it was so that pickpockets would not have the indecent temptation to fumble in the ladies' pockets.

♠ Nicolo Paganini liked to gamble. He once lost heavily before a concert and was forced to use his violin as a marker. A merchant, realizing the situation, loaned him a Guarneri *del Gesu*, but in the end gave him the violin as a gift. Another time Paganini bet he could play a difficult concert at sight without making a single mistake. The bet was over a Stradivari. He won.

♠ Mozart loved clothes, particularly lace, and gold watch chains.

♠ Gottschalk played hard, both at life and music. In the 1841-42 season, for instance, he gave 85 solo performances, mostly of his own music.

♠ Liszt learned music on the Esterhazy estate near Vienna where his father was estate manager. Years before Haydn had been music director there for about 30 years.

♠ *Amahl and the Night Visitors*, by Gian Carlo Menotti, made history as the first opera conceived and written for television. It was broadcast on Christmas Eve, 1951, on the NBC Television Network.

♠ In London in 1829, Mendelssohn received word from his uncle Nathan that the people of Silesia were in desperate need of help because of recent floods. He quickly organized a fundraiser for July 13, 1829. Big names performed. Rivals appeared on the same stage together, notably the Berlin soprano Henriette Sontag, and Maria Felicia Garcia, the contralto known as Malibran. The event was sold out.

♠ When Mozart and his father were returning to Salzburg from a three-year tour abroad, customs officials demanded duty on their gifts. Not about to part with the loot, a shrewd Papa Mozart brought out the clavier and asked his son to dazzle the crowd. The officials loved the music so much that they let them pass without paying the duty.

♠ In one of his financially lucrative periods in the 1780s in Vienna, Mozart's luxuries included a carriage and a horse for recreation. He also bought a forte piano with a specially constructed pedal attachment, a collection of other musical instruments, and a billiard table.

♠ Richard Wagner skipped school often. In 1829, the parents of the 15-year-old were informed that he had been absent from school for six months.

♠ Rossini's three greatest qualifications for a singer were: voice, voice and voice.

♠ Schubert's favorite American author was James Fennimore Cooper. In his last letter to his friend Franz Schober, dated November 11, 1828 (Schubert died on November 19th), Schubert said he was distressed and needed to read something. "Of Cooper's I have read *Last of the Mohicans*, *The Spy*, *The Pilot* and *The Pioneers*," he added. He also asked if there is more James Fennimore Cooper he could read.

♠ Stokowsky was conscious of his physical appearance at the podium, especially in the way his hands looked. Sometimes he had the lights in the hall illuminate them, creating intriguing shadows on the walls and the ceiling. In Hollywood, he insisted the camera hover over his hands, tracing their supple movements. Oscar Levant said, "I would like to be present, if I could have my choice of all the moments in musical history, at when Stokowsky suddenly became conscious of his beautiful hands. That must have been a moment."

♠ Verdi's *Aida*, commissioned in 1869 by the Khedive of Egypt to celebrate the opening of the Suez Canal, is the only opera in history connected with waterworks.

♠ Carl Maria Von Weber never conducted a concert without first dropping to his knees at the podium and praying.

♠ Artists have many unfinished works. Verdi did. His unfinished opera *Rochester* is lost. He wrote an overture for *The Barber of Seville*. Again vanished. He wrote two arias for *Faust*. Both gone.

♠ Mozart loved animals. He kept a little bird for three years, because it learned to whistle a tune from one of his concerti.

♠ Peter Ryom catalogued Vivaldi's music. The designation of RV before the catalogue number stands for Ryom Verzeichnis.

♠ In Vivaldi's time music piracy was a common practice, so many composers sold their composition directly to foreign visitors.

♠ When Schumann quit the University of Heidelberg, he headed to Leipzig where his law student friend Gisbert Rosen was. Along the way, he took a detour to Frankfurt. There, he stopped at a music shop and, claiming to be tutoring an English aristocrat in search of a good piano, chose the best instrument to test. For the next three hours the crowd was treated to a great show. Schumann then told the shop owner he would discuss the piano with his student and return in a couple of days. Only a couple of days later he was in Rudesheim drinking wine.

♠ Wagner's first orchestral piece was an overture. Since during scoring he had trouble distinguishing instrument parts, he used color codes: strings in red, woodwinds in green and brass in black. The piece flopped.

♠ The initial production of Franz Lehar's last operetta *Giuditta*, produced in 1934, was simulcast by 120 radio companies.

♠ Bedrich Smetana formed his own quartet in his early teens. Since the quartet had no money to buy music, Smetana would attend concerts around town with the idea of gathering music for the group to play. He listened to the music and then rushed home and copied it down on paper.

♠ Johann Strauss' wife Jetta had been urging him to write an operetta. One day she took a stack of unpublished manuscripts to the opera house without his knowledge. The manager brought in a librettist and they concocted an operetta. When Strauss found out about the conspiracy, he tried to suppress the work. "Only when you come up with something else," Strauss was told. Left without a choice, he came up with *The Merry Wives of Vienna*, which was rejected. His next operetta, *Indigo and the Forty Thieves*, was a smash, and Strauss was on his way as composer of delightful operettas.

♠ Queen Elizabeth I of England is usually credited with starting the practice of having music play while she dined.

♠ Mozart loved composing early in the morning and late at night. Usually he would compose from 6 to 9 a.m., then from 9 p.m. into the late hours. He kept to that schedule unless under a deadline.

♠ *The Grand Duchess of Gerolstein* was a smash hit at the 1867 World Exhibition in Paris. Ten million people saw the fair, including world leaders and dignitaries, 57 from royal families. Seats were sold out for the operetta and many royals booked early. The King of

Prussia saw it with Count Bismarck. The Czar of Russia had reserved seats for June. The Prince of Wales came in May and found the show sold out. Hortense Schneider, the star of the show, helped him see it by inviting him to her dressing room.

♠ The New York Philharmonic, America's oldest major orchestra, dates back to December 7, 1842. It started as a cooperative, with each musician contributing $25 to the general fund. Conductors and musicians divided the profits equally. The first season's take was $1,854.

♠ Schubert wrote 17 operas, but only three were performed in public. *Alfonso und Estrella* is his only grand opera.

♠ Handel's first opera *Almira* had 44 German and 15 Italian arias.

♠ Tchaikovsky, collaborating with his sister, wrote his first piece of music at age four. They wrote the piece for their mother, who was away in St. Petersburg to engage a governess, and titled it "Our Mama in Petersburg."

♠ Tchaikovsky was well recognized in Germany. One morning, after a particularly anti-Russian speech by Bismarck, a military band played under Tchaikovsky's hotel window. They even started the music with part of the Russian national anthem. Tchaikovsky stood at his window cold and embarrassed, but thankful for the honor. Soon other hotel guests appeared at their windows in various modes of dress, curious but undoubtedly enjoying the free entertainment.

♠ *Ospedale della Pieta'* were public schools in Italy for orphaned girls, where they received an excellent education and musical training. The girls expected to marry a middle class man afterward and enjoy a good life. Vivaldi headed one such school, for whose orchestra he wrote scores of concerti. The oldest school dated from 1346.

♠ Beethoven, who studied with Haydn for a short time, frustrated the master with his uncompromising ways, erratic moods and fits of temper. Later Haydn couldn't wait to be rid of him. Haydn was 60 and Beethoven 22. Known as gracious, generous and helpful, Haydn gave Ludwig a discount for his lessons and introduced him to people who could help him in his career. Beethoven, however, was ungrateful and deceitful toward the master, compelling Haydn to tell him: "You give me the impression of being a man who has several heads, several hearts and several souls." At first Beethoven mistook Haydn's intentions as self-serving, but years later he realized how wrong he had been in judging his teacher. Months before Haydn's death, at an event celebrating the master's achievements, Beethoven kissed Haydn's hand as the master was saying goodnight.

♠ Paganini, regarded as perhaps the greatest violinist, was flashy and a great showman. Sometimes he intentionally broke a violin string during performance and kept on playing. Or he cut three strings with scissors and created a miracle on the G String.

♠ Mendelssohn wrote letters to many people. On one occasion he wrote 27 long and detailed letters in one day.

♠ Mozart loved telling dirty jokes, which often embarrassed the family, his father in particular, since the old gent was a bit of a stuffed shirt.

♠ *Dafne*, written in 1627, is considered to be the first German opera, with a libretto by Martin Opitz and music by Heinrich Schutz.

♠ In 1927, Shostakovich won the first Chopin International Piano competition in Warsaw.

♠ *A Fiddle, a Sword and a Lady*, the 1953 novel by Albert Spaulding, the grocery chain owner, is based on the life of Giuseppe Tartini (1692-1770), who not only was a famous violinist and composer, but also a first class swordsman.

♠ The one opera Tchaikovsky truly loved was *Carmen* by Georges Bizet.

♠ John Field, the Irish composer and virtuoso pianist, is credited with having invented the musical form Nocturne. Later Chopin perfected it.

♠ In 1790, Haydn's 30-year career as music director for Prince Nicklas Esterhazy, who held court at Eisenstadt, a principality just over the Hungarian border, ended with the prince's death. Prince Anton, the son, could not afford the orchestra and disbanded it.

Haydn was given a pension of 1,400 florins, though he still remained in the Esterhazy service. At last Haydn was free. He even turned down a court music directorship position offered by King Ferdinand of Naples. He moved to Vienna.

♠ In 1809, the Hessian conductor Johann Friedrich Reichart calculated that on a given evening 50,000 Viennese danced in the small and great halls of the city, or one in four of Vienna's 200,000 inhabitants.

♠ In 1829, Mendelssohn arrived early for his concert in London's Argyll Rooms. Finding his piano locked, he improvised on an old standby and was so engrossed in playing that he failed to notice the audience drifting in. By then it was too late to practice on the piano he was supposed to play that evening. Nevertheless, the concert was well received. He wrote home that the hall was hot and the ladies wore colorful summer hats. He said he noticed their hats swayed in time to the music like a field of tulips.

♠ The Schuberts lived in a small apartment in Vienna. Since the father, Franz Theodore, was a schoolmaster who held classes in the family apartment, during the day 200 students were packed in, in two sessions, 100 in the morning and 100 in the afternoon. Later the family moved to a bigger house. *Good thinking.*

♠ "Someday you ought to stop fooling around with marches and write an operetta," Offenbach told John Philip Sousa, in 1876, at the International Exposition in Philadelphia. Sousa wrote several.

♠ In Tolstoy's *War and Peace*, the pianist who appears at Count Rostov's house supposedly has studied with John Field, the Irish pianist and composer.

♠ The 12-year-old Mendelssohn spent two precious weeks with the 72-year-old Goethe, who loved listening to the youngster play the piano. "I haven't heard you today," Goethe would say. "Make a little noise for me."

♠ The main reason why the audience sometimes stands during the "Hallelujah Chorus" from Handel's *Messiah* is because of what King George I started. He was so affected by the music that he shot to his feet in his box seat. Naturally the audience followed suit. Another story has it that King George often arrived late, entering his box just as the chorus broke into "Hallelujah." The audience naturally sprang to its feet with the king's arrival. So standing up for "Hallelujah Chorus" became the fashion.

♠ Liszt is generally regarded as the first pianist to perform from memory on the concert stage, and also the first to give a *master class*, as we know it today.

♠ Casanova (Giovanni Jacopo Casanova De Seingalt, 1725-1798) was a gambler and a spy as well as a playboy. He introduced the numbers racket to Paris, wrote science fiction stories, and played the violin. When Mozart was in Prague working on his opera *Don Giovanni*, Casanova tried to convince him that he, Casanova, was a far more colorful story for an opera than Don Juan. Mozart stuck with Don Juan.

♠ Francois Andre Philidor (1726-1795) was the first opera composer to have a curtain call.

♠ "Greensleeves," the English folk song, was first mentioned around 1580. At the turn of the 20th century, Ralph Vaughan Williams resurrected the tune, and since then it has been performed in every conceivable form.

♠ "The Star Spangled Banner," our National Anthem, goes back to Francis Scott Key's poem *The Defense of Fort McHenry*, which he later set to the music of "Anacreon in Heaven."

♠ Marie Antoinette's favorite instrument was the harp. For that reason, during her reign harp music became fashionable, and many composers wrote for it.

♠ The night before Mozart's opera *Don Giovanni* premiered in Prague, Mozart still had not written the overture. When the fuming theatre manager inquired where it was, Mozart told him not to worry about it. He tapped his forehead and announced, "In my head, all in my head, everything down to the last note." He asked the copyist to come by at 7 a.m., and began composing at midnight. All night his wife fed him punch and told stories to keep him from falling asleep.

Mozart did finish the overture at 7 a.m., and the copyist had it ready about a half hour before the performance that night. Since there was no time to rehearse, Mozart gave the downbeat and hoped for the best. *Don Giovanni* was a smash hit.

♠ The Blue Danube Waltz, written for the Men's Choral Society of Vienna, had such dreadful lyrics, by Josef Weyl, that the singers hated to sing them. The piece flopped. At the Paris Exhibition in 1867, Strauss and his orchestra played The Blue Danube Waltz for Prince Metternich without the lyrics. It was a smash hit. Soon all the other orchestras were playing the music. It became known as *The Waltz of Waltzes*, and the first piece of music in Paris to sell more than a million copies.

♠ Strauss became a hit at the 1872 International Peace Jubilee, held in Boston. He was so popular in America that on his walks six policemen were assigned to keep the crowds away. For one major event, Strauss organized an orchestra of 100 assistant conductors, 20,000 singers and 10,000 musicians. They performed for a crowd of 100,000.

♠ A song by Shostakovich was the first piece of music to be performed in space. On April 12, 1961, Yuri Gagarin, the first cosmonaut, sang it to mission control.

♠ Haydn, on his way to London in the company of the impresario Johann Solomon, stopped in Bonn, Beethoven's hometown. It was Saturday, December 25, 1790. He attended mass in the court chapel, where a mixed program of music was performed, including Haydn's own. By this time Haydn was revered. Toward the end of mass a gentleman informed Haydn and Solomon that they were expected in the oratory. The invitation had come from Elector Maximilian, who took Haydn by the hand and introduced him to the musicians. The elector then invited Haydn and Solomon to dinner at his palace. The unexpected invitation put Haydn in a precarious situation, since he and Solomon already had made plans for a small dinner at their hotel and it was too late to cancel. Haydn made his excuses and the elector graciously accepted. When Haydn and Solomon returned to the hotel, a big banquet was awaiting them. It seems the elector secretly changed that small dinner of theirs into a banquet for 12. It was a great surprise for Haydn. His dinner guests were musicians he had met at the court chapel, everything compliments of Elector Maximilian.

♠ The song "Erlkonig" ("Earl King"), one of Schubert's most famous songs, set to Goethe's poem, was written in one sitting. Schubert was waiting for his friends Spaun and Mayerhofer when the poem popped in his head.

♠ Richard Strauss loved drinking beer and playing a card game called *Skat*. He got his ideas that way, including the waltz melody for his opera *Der Rosenkavalier*.

♠ As a young pianist, Brahms toured for a short time with the gypsy violinist Eduard Remenyi. At a place near Hanover one night, they discovered the piano was tuned half a note too low. They were playing Beethoven's Sonata in C Minor, Op. 30 No. 2, among other things. Remenyi refused to tune down his violin, fearing the performance would lose brilliance. Without hesitating, Brahms started a half a tone up, and they played the piece in C-sharp minor. The performance apparently was lovely.

♠ Franz Von Suppe was the nephew of Gaetano Donizetti.

♠ In a music class one day Tchaikovsky wrote over 200 variations on a given theme.

♠ The first time the Wedding March – from *A Midsummer Night's Dream* by Mendelssohn – was played at a wedding was in 1858, when Queen Victoria's daughter Royal married the crown prince of Prussia.

♠ Queen Victoria liked Mendelssohn's *Songs Without Words*. The ones she liked most, however, were those written by Mendelssohn's sister Fanny and published under his name.

♠ Mozart, a regular guest of a certain Von Kees who held frequent musicals in his home in Vienna, would always write songs for the host's wife to sing. One day Mozart was nowhere to be seen, so they dispatched the servant to find him. The servant found Mozart in a saloon. Having forgotten about the event, and the promised song for the lady, Mozart sent the servant for a sheet of paper and then wrote a song in a few minutes, taking it with him to the party.

♠ In the 1830s, scores of useless mechanical devices were sold to pianists to strengthen their hands. Schumann fell for such a device. Another story claims that he invented a little sling that restrained one finger while he exercised the others. Either way, he ruined his budding career as a concert pianist by damaging two tendons in his right hand. One contradicting story, however, places the blame on venereal disease that he had contracted in his youth. At the time patients were treated with mercury, which damages the nervous system. It apparently did Schumann's. Venereal disease is also partly responsible for his death, it is said.

♠ Young Tchaikovsky was always tinkering at the piano, or tapping tunes on the windowpane while staring out. He got carried away once and broke the window glass, cutting his hand.

♠ Mozart was the main reason Tchaikovsky decided to devote his life to music. While staying in St. Petersburg with Modest Alexevich Vakar, a family friend, Tchaikovsky saw Mozart's opera *Don Giovanni*. That became the turning point in his life. Mozart dazzled him. From then on music became his life and Mozart his favorite composer.

♠ Gabriel Faure became composer by chance. He was playing the harmonium in a chapel near his school when a blind woman heard him. She was so impressed that she told his father about the boy's talent. His father took him to the *Ecole Niedermeyer* to study the organ. Later Faure took piano lessons from Saint-Saens.

♠ In *La Boheme*, the bass Andres de Seguerola suddenly lost his voice. He turned to Caruso and in panic pantomimed, "No voice." Caruso, cool and calm, whispered, "Make the words with your lips and I will sing for you from the back." So Caruso darkened his voice and gave a fairly good imitation of the bass in the "Coal Song."

♠ Lully angered King Louis XIV, his boss, over an argument. Realizing his predicament, Lully tried everything at a performance to make the king happy, including playing the king's favorite music. Nothing worked. Finally, out of desperation, he wound up his feet and plopped right on the harpsichord, smashing it. Louis cracked up laughing, and all was forgiven.

♠ Mendelssohn's son Paul, who lived to be only 38, founded *Agfa*, which became the well-known photographic business.

♠ Mendelssohn was generous in promoting young talent. When heading the Leipzig Conservatory of Music, he offered scholarships to students and provided free private lessons for the poor students. One 12-year-old prodigy was especially grateful to the master, as Mendelssohn helped him, encouraged him, and even accompanied him to concerts. That kid grew up to be one of the greatest violinists in history – the Hungarian Joseph Joachim.

♠ In 1839, Franz Liszt invented the concept of the solo concert *recital* – as we know it today – because he wanted the stage all to himself. At first he called his solo appearances *soliloquies*, and later changed them to *recitals*. In 1840, Liszt puzzled Londoners who had never heard the term *recital*. What did he mean? How can anyone *recite* upon the pianoforte? Always the great showman, at these *recital*s Liszt would play a piece from the program, stop and mingle with the audience, and then return to the stage to resume the concert.

♠ Verdi scored his first success at age 29 with the opera *Nabucco*.

♠ In the later years in Vienna, Haydn's daily routine was this: He rose at 6:30 a.m. While dressing, he worked with a student. Breakfast was at 8. He sketched compositions at the piano until 11:30. For the next two hours he received visitors, or paid calls, or went for a walk. He dined from 2 to 3 p.m. From then until 8 o'clock he attended to domestic matters and scored his sketches from that morning. At 8 he went out for about an hour or so. Then he orchestrated more music, and read until about 10. He had a light supper of bread and wine, unless invited to dine out. Finally he went to bed at 11:30 p.m. This routine remained the same until the later years when his health began to fail.

♠ The Esterhazys were nobility dating back two centuries. The Esterhazy men had married rich, usually more than once, and continued to amass a fortune. At one time the Esterhazys owned 25 castles and about 1.5 million acres of land. During the rule of the Hapsburgs, the Esterhazys became palatines of Hungary. Prince Nickolas was a cultured man, with his own orchestra and theatre. For almost 30 years Haydn directed all the musical activities for the Esterhazys. At the Eisenstadt estate, Haydn, whose official start date was May 1, 1761, would present himself to the prince for instructions on the day's musical activities. His high position still did not preclude Haydn from being regarded as a servant, where he had to adhere to the court's rules of dress, conduct and culture. And his life had to be free of scandal.

♠ Caruso had a special recipe to get his throat ready for singing. He would sniff a pinch of Swedish snuff to clear his nostrils; then gargle with lukewarm saltwater, followed by a sip of diluted whisky.

♠ During a two-week period with the Philadelphia Orchestra, Stokowsky had the librarian keep a certain work handy for rehearsal to accommodate a player who was an expectant father. The score called for him to play at the beginning and at the end, leaving 500 bars of rest in between. When word came from the hospital, Stokowsky asked for the score. The musician played his first part before dashing out to the hospital, all the while counting the measures. He saw his baby, kissed his wife and returned to the Academy of Music just in time to play the finale.

♠ After watching George Sand's Pekinese dog Chow-Chow chasing its tail, Chopin suddenly laughed and ambled to the piano. A short time later he had composed one of his most famous miniature: Waltz in Db (*Minute Waltz*).

♠ Archangelo Corelli was relatively wealthy but a cheapskate, who skimped on food, clothing and lodging. He always wore black. "Corelli has a veritable passion for visiting art galleries on those days when there is no admission," said Handel, also noting that Corelli collected art for which he never paid.

♠ Dvorak, who was a daydreamer, once faded out completely while conducting his *Stabat Mater*. It took a smack on the head from the concertmaster's bow to snap him out of it.

♠ In his early years, Joseph Lanner played in Michael Pamer's orchestra. Pamer had a shtick in that he would guzzle stein after stein of beer on stage, goaded by his audience. In 1819, Lanner founded a quartet with Johann Strauss Sr. The popular quartet broke up when Lanner and Strauss parted ways, eventually to become rivals.

♠ On October 4, 1835, Mendelssohn's first concert as music director of the Gewandhaus Orchestra of Leipzig raised eyebrows. Until then, the concertmaster, or the leader, would perform standing and relaying the signals to the orchestra. Mendelssohn changed that practice by making the concertmaster sit and he himself stood at the podium with a slim whalebone baton in hand, much in the way conductors conduct today.

♠ One of the famous portraits of Haydn painted in London by John Hoppner now hangs at Buckingham Palace. Haydn, a jovial person with a ready smile, loved a good conversation. Yet the moment he sat for an artist, he turned stiff and wooden. Hoppner found an idea to cure the situation. He had Haydn's German chambermaid sit across from the composer and talk to him. The strategy worked and Haydn relaxed.

♠ One of Tchaikovsky's grandfathers, several notches up the family tree, was a Cossack officer.

♠ It was an emergency and Donizetti was given two weeks to write an opera. Unaccustomed to patching up old operas, he opted to write a new one. He gave his librettist Felice Romani one week to write. "It must be set to music within fourteen days," Donizetti said. "Let's see which of us has guts." That opera was *L'Elisir d'Amore*.

♠ Sir Edward Elgar's Pomp and Circumstance March No. 1, often heard at graduation ceremonies in the US, was first played in London in 1890. The audience shot to its feet with cheers and applause. When the orchestra played it again, the audience had the same reactions. It was played one more round before the orchestra continued with the rest of the program.

♠ The autocratic conductor Arturo Toscanini, who during rehearsals frequently lost his temper, sometimes would snap his baton to pieces in anger. On one occasion, the baton wouldn't break, so he turned his anger at his handkerchief, but it wouldn't tear. At last, the furious Toscanini removed his coat and tore it to shreds. When done, he took a breath and announced, "We shall take it again."

♠ Gabriel Faure, as head of the Paris Conservatory of Music, was concerned for the dignity of his position, so he would get off the Metro one station before his stop and take a cab to the conservatory.

♠ Liszt was invited to Mendelssohn's party, and he went dressed in Hungarian national clothing and looking wild and handsome. He was invited to play. Following a Hungarian folk song and some variations, he insisted Mendelssohn play. "Well, I will play," said Mendelssohn, "but you mustn't get angry with me." He played the same Hungarian folk song Liszt had played, with the same variations, and the same way, from memory. He also imitated Liszt's grandiose movements and extravagant gestures. For those few minutes, the conservative Mendelssohn was as flashy as Liszt. Liszt laughed and applauded. He said he could not have copied himself so accurately.

♠ Caruso once was arrested for pinching a woman in the monkey house at the Central Park Zoo in New York.

♠ In 1783, Jan Ladislav Dussek was in St. Petersburg in the court of Catherine II when implicated in a plot against her. He fled to Lithuania, where he became music director for Prince Karl Radziwill. From 1786 until 1789, Dussek worked for Marie Antoinette in Paris, writing lovely harp music for her, until the French Revolution forced him to flee to London. In 1792, he married Sophia Corri, who became famous as harpist, pianist and singer. Dussek joined his father-in-law's music publishing business, which soon became known as Corri, Dussek and Company. When the firm sank into debt, Dussek fled to Hamburg, leaving the old man to go to jail. Eventually Dussek wrote to Sophia, but no one knows if he ever saw her again, or their daughter Olivia.

♠ Brahms met the Russian novelist Ivan Turgenev and his female companion, the singer Pauline Viardot, as they traveled through Europe. They became friends. Turgenev offered to collaborate with Brahms on an opera. Sadly, they did not write it.

♠ Medical school horrified the young Berlioz. Seeing a corpse in the dissecting room and the rats nibbling at the scraps was enough to make him jump out the window and run straight to the Paris Conservatory. *No doctoring for him.*

♠ Beethoven liked to pour cold water on his hands before composing at the piano. He said it helped him think.

♠ Pigeon breeding was Dvorak's favorite hobby.

♠ Because he was in the Nazi party during WWII, after the war conductor Herbert Von Karajan was forbidden to conduct for two years. When he brought the Berlin Philharmonic to America for the 1954-55- season tour, violent demonstrations broke out against his visit.

♠ Geraldine Farrar's father in the 1880s was a major league baseball player.

♠ Some conductors and musicians sent locks of hair from their dog rather than from them to their lady fans. One such conductor was Arthur Nikisch (1855-1922).

♠ By 1740, his name faded and his wealth gone, Vivaldi moved to Vienna, at the time the center of music. Emperor Charles VI, with whom Vivaldi had developed a friendship, invited him to his court. When Charles VI died unexpectedly that year, his daughter, Maria Theresa, ascended the throne. Maria Theresa was not disposed toward Vivaldi, so he was left without a patron. He died in Vienna 1741, destitute, and was buried in a pauper's grave.

♠ Toscanini was known for his phenomenal memory. Before a concert once, a clarinetist came to him, lamenting that he had broken his E-natural key and would be unable to play that night. Toscanini closed his eyes for a moment and said, "It's all right. You don't have an E-natural tonight."

♠ In 1903, when Fritz Kreisler visited Dvorak in his home in Prague, he found him ill and broke. Kreisler asked if he had anything for him to play on the violin. Dvorak said to look through the pile of manuscripts in the corner. There, Kreisler found "Humoresque," the miniature that became one of Dvorak's most famous pieces of music.

♠ Brahms' affection for tin soldiers carried into old age. He would often bring out his collection for friends' children, set them up and move them around.

♠ Bizet had a passion for literature, but his father wanted him to be a musician. So the old man hid all the books in the house and made Georges practice the piano all day.

♠ Bizet began some 30 operas, but completed only seven.

♠ Brahms loved Bizet's opera *Carmen* so much that he saw it 20 times.

♠ In Spain, *Carmen* was performed in a bullring, with a real matador and a bull.

♠ The composer Saint-Saens was looking for Bizet one day. Not sure where Bizet lived, Saint-Saens walked up and down the street, which got him nowhere. Finally he began singing an aria from Bizet's opera *Pearl Fishers*. Bizet heard the singing. *Hel-l-l-l-l-o.*

♠ Rosa Ponselle and the Metropolitan Opera had a disagreement: she liked to ride her bicycle to rehearsals and the Met disapproved. The Met threatened to include that discussion in her contract. *I don't know who won that argument.*

♠ Benjamino Gigli was once an apprentice in a tailor shop.

♠ Mr. Fashion Beethoven was not. He would forget to change his shirt, or trousers, and would wear the same things day after day. He once looked so ragged that the police mistook him for a bum and threw him in the calaboose.

♠ Dvorak and his wife, both early risers, were guests of the English composer Charles Villiers Stanford. One morning Stanford heard noise in the garden. It was 6 a.m. He looked out the window into the yard and saw the Dvoraks sitting under a tree. Stanford was put out by their lifelong habit as early risers.

♠ Visiting his hometown of Hamburg, Germany, Brahms went to the house where he once had lived. He stood motionless in his room, lost in thought, and then suddenly began peeling off the wallpaper. He was looking for the manuscripts he had used to cover the cracks in the walls.

♠ The young Beethoven played in the orchestra at the court chapel in Bonn, where Christmas was celebrated with pageantry. The formal dress for the musicians, including Beethoven, was as follows: tail coat sea-green in color, short green knee-breeches with buckles, white or black silk stockings, shoes with black bows, and white flowered silk waistcoat with flap pockets. The waistcoat was bordered with pure gold cord. Hair dressed in curls and pigtail. A cocked hat under the left arm and sword on the left hip hung with a silver sword belt.

♠ Wagnerian singer Kirsten Flagstad, late in her life, recorded *Tristan und Isolde* soaring with her high Cs, the same notes she had repeatedly missed on the stage. That's because someone else' high Cs were dubbed in – Elizabeth Schwarzkopf's.

♠ Brahms always found something to admire and enjoy in rain and drizzle. "I never feel it dull," he said. "My view is so fine. Even when it rains, I have only another kind of beauty."

♠ The violinist Joseph Joachim, Brahms' old friend, gave this description of Brahms: "Brahms has a dual personality: one is mostly a naïve genius, the other devilishly cunning, which with a frosty surface suddenly explodes in pedantic, prosaic need to dominate."

♠ The French conductor Louis Antoine Julienne always conducted Beethoven wearing white gloves. In his early promenade concerts in the 1840s London, he conducted Beethoven with a variety of instrumentation. For the *Pastoral* Symphony's thunderstorm movement, he tried to create nature's sound by shaking a tin box filled with dried peas, this in addition to the sound effects the orchestra created.

♠ Bach had many collaborators, including Christian Friedrich Unold, the author of *St. Mathew Passion*. Unold was later run out of town for writing pornography.

♠ Ernestine Schumann-Heinke had sons fighting on both sides in WWI. The son fighting for the Germans was killed.

♠ Beethoven had three ancient Egyptian inscriptions under glass on his desk: (1) I am that which is. (2) I am everything that is, that was, and that will be. No mortal man has lifted my veil. (3) He is of himself alone, and it is to this aloneness that all things owe their being.

♠ Beethoven wrote "Fur Elise" for his young student Elise Keyser. He had promised her a fur piece if she were nice to him. She was. So he gave her the tune instead.

♠ Luigi Lablache, who gave singing lessons to Victoria before she became queen of England, was famous for his breath control. He once sang a long note from soft to loud and back to soft, drank a glass of water, sang a chromatic scale up the octave in trills, and finally blew out a candle with his mouth open – all in a single breath.

♠ Dietrich Fischer-Dieskau, the renowned singer of lieder, was an American prisoner of war in Italy at the end of WWII.

♠ Stephan Mallarme, the French poet who wrote *Afternoon of a Faun* – which Debussy illustrated in music as Prelude to the Afternoon of a Faun – loved Edgar Allen Poe so much that he learned English just to read him in the original language.

♠ Bach was so frugal that he once wrote a whole flute sonata just because he had three empty staves left over at the bottom of a concerto.

♠ Pablo Casals, the great Catalan cellist, began each day for more than 70 years by playing Bach. Casals also practiced Bach's six cello suites for 12 years before performing them in public.

♠ In the time of Haydn, Mozart and Beethoven, concerts were often interrupted, usually after the second movement of a symphony, when the management brought on stage an instrumentalist or a singer to entertain. After the interlude, the scheduled program would continue. It was thought that no audience could survive the intellectual pressure of something like a Beethoven symphony straight through.

♠ Catherine the Great, on ascending the Russian throne, commissioned an opera using her own libretto. The opera was titled *Minerva's Triumph*. It took two weeks to perform. It flopped.

The Empress wrote two more operas: *The Early Reign of Oleg, the Varangian*, and *Bulaevich, the Novgorodian Hero*. Both flopped. So old Cathy gave up writing operas and stuck to being queen.

♠ In the late 1700s and early 1800s, battle music, composed to glorify battles, became fashionable in Europe. The music was given elaborate titles. One in particular probably has the longest title: "The Battle of Wurzburg on the Third of September, 1796, Between the Royal Imperial Army Under the Command of His Imperial Highness the Archduke Karl of Austria, Imperial Field Marshall, and the Enemy French Troops Under the Command of General Jourdan" – by Mr. Johann Wanhal.

♠ National anthems have lyrics, except for those of Bahrain and Qatar, which are straight instrumentals.

♠ During the run of the opera *Cleopatra* in Hamburg, the 19-year-old Handel and the opera's composer Matheson got into a fight over who should take over at the harpsichord in the final scene. The disagreement led to a fistfight, with the audience watching, and culminated into a sword fight. At one point Matheson lunged at Handel with his sword and, luckily, only caught a button. *Hallelujah, brothers and sisters!*

♠ Just before Custer led his troops out of Fort Lincoln heading for the Little Big Horn, the band played the 7th Cavalry's battle tune – "Gary Owen."

♠ Beethoven was forgetful. Often he forgot to eat, or tried to pay for food he had not eaten in cafes. He once soaped his face to shave and, forgetting about it, walked around Vienna all day with shaving soap on his face. Sometimes his friends would replace his old and tattered clothing in his closet with something new. Beethoven would wear it without the slightest idea it was new.

♠ In 1703, Vivaldi was ordained into the priesthood, but soon he retired from office for a number of reasons. Having suffered from lung problems, he was often confined to his home. Because of this, while conducting mass, he would often run out of breath. Also, his extensive musical training was another reason to leave the priesthood.

♠ Haydn was born in Rohrau in eastern Austria on April 1, 1732. He himself said he was born on the night of March 31, 1732. "My brother Michael preferred to claim that I was born on 31 March," said Haydn, "because he did not want people to say I had come into the world as an April fool."

♠ That Wagner was an anti-Semite is known. He also disliked the French, because, as a young man, he had spent a hard year in Paris trying to produce one of his operas and failed.

♠ Although Tchaikovsky and Brahms were acquainted, they failed to strike a great friendship. They were honest and open about disliking one another's music.

What's yours is mine

Or the jolly art of borrowing

*C*omposers have been notorious for borrowing – or stealing – music from others. Composers of film music, especially, have mastered the jolly art of borrowing. I admit that some similarities between compositions might be inadvertent. Take the song "Stormy Weather," which Harold Arlen and Ted Kohler wrote for the 1933 Cotton Club Revue, and the Adagio of Spartacus and Phrygia, which Aram Khachaturian wrote for the 1954 ballet *Spartacus*. Whether Khachaturian borrowed from Arlen, I wouldn't know. I can only point to the amazing resemblance in the two pieces of music. On the other hand, maybe after all the years behind the microphone I hear things.

♠ A famous Hollywood composer was commissioned to write a 500-page film score on a tight deadline. "That will take a lot out of you, won't it?" asked a friend. "Oh, no," replied the composer. "Not out of me, but out of Tchaikovsky, Dvorak and Sibelius."

♠ When Handel was caught stealing music from Giovanni Bononcini, he shrugged and said, "It was too good for Bononcini."

♠ The United State Marine Corps has Offenbach to thank for the Marine's famous hymn "The Halls of Mentezuma." The melody is derived from the martial tune titled "Couplets des Hommes de l'Armee" from the operetta *Genevieve de Brabant*.

♠ *Le Papillon*, Offenbach's only full-length ballet, choreographed by Marie Taglioni, includes a charming waltz tune at the beginning of the second act. The French songwriter George Leybourne arranged it into the popular song "The Daring Young Man On a Flying Trapeze." Strauss also used Offenbach's tune.

♠ Fritz Kreisler, the Austrian-born violinist and composer, claimed that in 1909 he had discovered 53 manuscripts by past masters in a monastery in Avignon, France, and had them published for $8,000. In 1935, he confessed to having written all the pieces himself, and that he took the names from the Groves Dictionary. The confession caused a big scandal. He further claimed that the music he had found was not all for violin, and that he arranged some of the pieces, making minor changes in the melodies, but retaining the spirit of the original works.

♠ While working on the movie *Fantasia,* Stokowsky suggested to Walt Disney that they film Bach's composition Toccata and Fugue. "Fine," said Disney. "You take care of the music and let our writers worry over what story to use."

♠ In 1944, the Universal Studio in Hollywood was working on *Christmas Holiday,* starring Deanna Durbin and Gene Kelley. *Liebestodt* from Wagner's opera *Tristan und Isolde* is heard at the end of the movie. The producer, wanting the score to sound classical, told the composer to make it sound like Wagner – only louder.

♠ "Midnight Bells" from the operetta *The Opera Ball,* composed in 1898 by the Austrian composer Richard Heurberger, was used under the title "The Bell Waltz" as the opening theme for *The Telephone Hour,* a radio program that began at midnight on the Mutual Broadcasting Company.

♠ The Arabian Dance from Tchaikovsky's Christmas Holiday ballet *The Nutcracker* is based on a Georgian folk tune.

♠ Samuel Goldwyn was planning a movie that would be set in what was then Czechoslovakia. Screenwriter Ben Hecht and composer George Antheil urged him to hire Ernst Krenek to write the score. Krenek was in Hollywood, and broke. "Never heard of him," said Goldwyn. "What has he written?" Hecht and Antheil rattled off a list of Krenek's music, none of which Goldwyn had heard. "And he wrote *The Threepenny Opera* and *Rosenkavalier,*" embellished Antheil. "And *Faust* and *La Traviata,*" Hecht chimed in. "So he wrote *La Traviata,* did he?" snapped Goldwyn. "Well, just bring him around so's I can get my hands on him. Why, his publishers almost ruined me with a lawsuit just because we used a few bars of that lousy opera. We had to retake half of the picture for a few lousy bars." Of course, Krenek did not get the job.

♠ *La Traviata* (The Castaway) is based on the novel *The Girl of the Camellias* by Alexandre Dumas, the younger. The story is based on the life of Marie Alphonsine Duplessis (1824-1847), a beautiful prostitute who was Dumas' lover for 11 months. She died at 23 and is buried at the Montmartre Cemetery in Paris. Marie Duplessis always wore a Camellia, and even to this day people put Camellias on her grave. She was a 16-year-old laundress when a wealthy baron took her as a mistress. In her short life she had many lovers, including Liszt. What's ironic is that Liszt was warned to keep away from her to guard his reputation – *and Liszt was anything but a eunuch.*

♠ Tchaikovsky found music everywhere. While scoring his opera *Ondine*, he overheard a carpenter singing a lovely folk song. It was this song that he made famous as the Andante Cantabile movement from his String Quartet No. 1.

♠ A Hollywood producer, working on a French comedy, wanted the score to have greater lightness and deftness, so he insisted the composer use more French horns to get the sound.

♠ Agnes Kimball first recorded "Un Bel Dei," from *Madama Butterfly*, in English, in 1912. It was also sung in the 1939 movie *First Love* with Robert Stack and Deana Durbin. Durbin sang it in English.

♠ Omphale's Spinning Wheel, composed by Camille Saint-Saens, is a little tone poem that depicts the enslavement of Hercules by Omphale, Queen of Lydia. The music was used throughout the old time radio show *The Shadow*.

♠ A Hollywood producer jumped with joy that a projected movie would use Brahms' "Cradle Song" as a leitmotif. "This will be a Class A production," he declared. "We must get Brahms himself to come to Hollywood to write the whole score."

♠ Handel wrote about 46 operas. When he ran out of ideas, sometimes he would take something old and give it a new title.

♠ *Casablanca* was adapted from an unsuccessful play titled *Everybody Comes to Rick's*. The song "As Time Goes By" was written by Herman Hupfeld for the 1931 review titled *Everybody's Welcome*. Max Steiner adapted the song for *Casablanca*.

♠ *The Magic Bow*, the 1947 movie about Paganini, starred Stewart Granger as Paganini, with Phyllis Calvert, Gene Kent and David Price. Yehudi Menuhin played all the violin music by Paganini that was used in the movie.

♠ In 1923, Vincent Youmans composed the musical *No, No, Nannette*. The best number out of the show was the fox trot "Tea For Two." Everyone loved it in Russia, where it became known as "Tahiti Trot." Shostakovich was traveling in the Ukraine with his friend, the conductor Nikolai Malko, when they heard "Tahiti Trot" on the gramophone. "Well, Mitenka," said Malko. "If you have as much genius as they say you do, I give you one hour to go into the next room, put down that little piece on paper from memory and orchestrate it for me to play." Shostakovich did it in 45 minutes.

♠ *Romance* in the 1955 film *The Gadfly*, composed by Dmitri Shostakovich, was used as the theme for the PBS TV series *Riley Ace of Spies* with Sam Neal.

♠ In 1880, Josef Ivanovici, a Romanian military bandleader, composed the waltz Danube Waves. In 1946, Al Jolson and Sol Chaplin adapted the music as the "Anniversary Song" for the movie *The Jolson Story*.

♠ Chopin's Etude in C Minor, Op. 10 No. 12 (*Revolutionary*) expressed his anger after the Russians captured Warsaw, in 1831. In the movie *Song to Remember*, Cornel Wild, playing the Chopin etude (Jose Iturbe did the actual playing), bleeds on the piano keyboard. People then began referring to the piece as the "Ketchup On The Key Etude."

Death does not blow a trumpet

A Danish proverb

Throw a mystery my way and I charge like a hooting Mongol warrior. I did at the so-called poisoning of Mozart by Salieri. Sure, scholars refute the claim, but who cares? It's a great yarn. Alexander Pushkin thought so when he wrote his play *Mozart and Salieri*. Of course Pushkin himself was killed in a duel. Extraordinary deaths abound in the classical music world. Here are some I came across, but I am sure a lot more stories exist. Since I could not resist other instances of death in the classical music world, I have thrown them in for good measure.

♠ While working on his *Requiem*, Mozart began speaking of death, noting that he was writing the piece for himself. He said he knew he wouldn't last long. "I'm sure I have been poisoned," he said. "I cannot rid myself of this idea." Years later, his wife Constanza confided in friends that, in later years, Mozart was impressed with the horrid idea that someone had poisoned him. According to some authorities, the imagined sensation of having poison in his body might have been a medical symptom of the disease that eventually took his life. Toward the end he was always tired, lethargic and melancholic. It is now widely accepted that he died of acute rheumatic fever.

♠ The rumor about Antonio Salieri (1750-1825) poisoning Mozart started when Salieri said, "A genius has departed. Let's all rejoice, for soon no one would have given us a piece of bread for our own music." Salieri is suspected of having feared, hated and envied Mozart. Years later, when he lay dying in the poor wing of Vienna's general hospital, he told his pupil, the pianist and composer Ignaz Moscheles, "I am finished, but before I go, I want you to know and to tell it to the world that I did not poison Mozart."

♠ Speaking with Salieri, Rossini jokingly said, "It's lucky for Beethoven that his instinct for self-preservation leads him to avoid dining with you. Otherwise you might pack him off to the next world, as you did Mozart." Salieri replied, "Do I look like a poisoner?"

♠ Johann Schobert (1735-1767) died by eating poison mushrooms.

♠ The murder of the French composer Jean-Marie Leclaire – also one of the greatest violinists of the baroque – is worthy of Dorothy Sayers. Leclaire was murdered in his home as he returned late one evening. *The usual suspects* included his gardener. So did Leclaire's estranged wife Louise. Evidence in the French National Archives, though, apparently seems to points to Leclaire's nephew, the violinist Guillaume-Francois Vial, since they had been feuding. A bigger mystery is that Vial was never brought to trial.

♠ Mussolini delivered the eulogy at Puccini's funeral.

♠ A woman blackmailed Tchaikovsky over the relationship he had with her son. At the time a cholera epidemic ravaged Moscow. For many years after, Tchaikovsky's death was attributed to drinking contaminated water. Later it was discovered that he poisoned himself over this relationship and its public consequences. At Tchaikovsky's deathbed, his brothers Modest and Nikolay were present, as were his nephew Bob Davidov, a cousin, and a friend of Bob's, three doctors, and his longtime beloved servant Alexey Sofranov. His brother Modest recalled that at the last moment Tchaikovsky looked about him and seemed to recognize everyone; then he closed his eyes.

♠ Leonardo Vinci (c.1690-1730) was poisoned by his mistress.

♠ In the case of the Italian baroque composer Alessandro Stradella, it was chasing all those wenches that finally *done* him in. Stradella took off with Alvide Contarini's mistress. Contarini, a Venetian senator, sent 40 of his boys after Stradella, but they managed only to wound him, and he escaped. He was not so lucky after romancing a young lady from the powerful Lomellini family in Genoa. Stradella was ambushed one late night in the Piazza Bianchi and killed. Was it the Lomellinis who were responsible for the hit, or old Contarini, or was it another avenging man whose woman Stradella had stolen? No one knows who gave the order to whack him.

♠ When Chopin died, Berlioz declared, "Ah, he was dying all his life." While living, Chopin had cared very little for Berlioz.

♠ Louis Moreau Gottschalk collapsed at the piano while performing in Rio de Janeiro. The piece he was playing was called "*Morte.*" He died a short while later of apparently peritonitis, at age 40. Numerous rumors about the cause of his death include murder by some husband whose wife had had an affair with Gottschalk. The composer's remains were interred with great ceremony in Brooklyn, NY, on October 3, 1870.

♠ Charles Valentine Alkan (1813-1888) died when a bookcase toppled over him.

♠ Emma Livry (1842-1863), the French prima ballerina, was rehearsing a ballet called *Zara*, choreographed by Marie Taglioni, when tragedy struck. At the time Paris had a regulation that all dancer costumes had to be treated with a fireproof solution. Livry refused to comply, because the costume became too stiff. She even signed a note that absolved the management from responsibility. On November 15, 1862, her skirt touched a gaslight on the stage and flames engulfed her body. Livry was burned badly and died eight months later after much suffering.

♠ Alexander Pushkin (1799-1837) was killed in a duel.

♠ Mikhail Lermontov (1814-1841) was killed in a duel.

♠ Ernest Chausson (1855-1899) died in a bicycle accident.

♠ Ceasar Franck (1822-1890) was run over by a bus.

♠ Alban Berg (1885-1935) died of an insect bite.

♠ In 1838, Chopin was in Majorca with George Sand. He was ill with tuberculosis. "The three most celebrated doctors on the island have seen me," he said. "One sniffed at what I spat. The second tapped where I spat. The third sounded me and listened as I spat. The first said I was dead, the second that I am dying and that third that I am going to die."

♠ When John Field lay dying, an English clergyman asked if he was a Protestant. "No," said Field. "Perhaps a Catholic," said the clergyman. "No," said Field. "Then you must be a Calvinist," said the clergyman. "Not quite," answered Field. "I am a clavicinist."

♠ Anton Filtz (1730-1760), composer and virtuoso cellist, was one of the most important symphonists of the Manheim School of composers and musicians. He died from eating a poisonous spider. Claiming spiders tasted like strawberries, and had a special recipe for cooking them — story goes that he liked to sauté them with mushrooms and garlic.

♠ Shortly after Beethoven's death (1770-1827), a caretaker heard faint music coming from the crypt. Four notes were repeated in the same pattern – a long note followed by three short notes a major third higher. The police came, and a priest, and a musicologist, and they all fanned around Beethoven's grave, ears to the headstone. Once again the sounds were there. "That's the Fifth Symphony theme backward," announced the scholar, laughing. "Beethoven is decomposing."

♠ Stephen Foster (1826-1864) died after a fall in a New York rooming house.

♠ After the 100th performance of *Orpheus in the Underworld*, the cast gathered in Offenbach's courtyard at 1 a.m. and sang chorus after chorus from the operetta. Then everyone marched upstairs and presented Offenbach with a gilded wreath. When the cast asked Offenbach's neighbor, an ailing elderly lady who lived on the first floor of the apartment, if she objected to all the hoopla, she answered no. "I should not wonder if it prolongs my life," she added.

♠ Fritz Wunderlich (1930-1966) died from a fall down the stairs.

♠ As court music director for Louis XIV, Jean-Babtist Lully (1632 -1687) had political clout that included controlling the musical life of Paris. That's why his enemies kept trying to bump him off. One went so far as to spike Lully's tobacco with arsenic. But Lully survived all that, only to die from an infection after stabbing his foot with his conductor's staff.

♠ Rossini was a leap-year baby, born February 29, 1792. The superstitious Rossini dreaded Fridays and the Number 13 – and he died on Friday the 13th.

♠ Jeremiah Clark (1673-1707), composer and organist at St. Paul's Cathedral in London, fell in love with a noblewoman, but was rejected by her. The desperate Clark decided to end his life. The question was how to do it, hang himself, drown himself, what? He tossed a coin. The coin landed on clay soil, on its edge, so Clark shot himself.

♠ Alberic Magnard (1865-1914), the French composer, was killed by the German soldiers he shot at from the window of his home when they entered his property.

♠ Karel Komzak (1850-1905), the bandleader and composer of waltzes, was killed while attempting to jump on board a moving train.

♠ One night in November 1695, Henry Purcell (1659-1695) returned home from a party after his curfew of midnight and discovered his wife had locked him out. It was a cold and rainy night. He caught a cold while walking up and down the street in front of the house all night and died a few days later, at age 36.

♠ Following Chopin's death, his sister Ludwika took his heart to Warsaw, to the Holy Cross Church. Chopin is buried in Paris.

♠ Tragedies in his youth marked Schumann for life. His 19-year-old sister, Emilie, depressed because of her acute skin disease, committed suicide by drowning. His father, August, was crushed by her death and a few weeks later he died. Schumann, therefore, developed such fear of death and funerals that he stayed away from his mother's funeral, in 1836. Later he would try suicide, but fail. He died in an insane asylum in 1856.

♠ Leonard Warren (1911-1960) died on the stage of the Metropolitan Opera while singing in Verdi's *La Forza del Destino* (The Force of Destiny).

♠ At Beethoven's funeral, a passing stranger asked a woman what was going on. "Well, don't you know?" she answered. "The general of the musicians has died."

♠ Beethoven's funeral was on the afternoon of March 29, 1827. By then he was revered all over the civilized world. The ceremony was one of the most spectacular in post-Napoleonic Vienna. Twenty thousand people marched in the procession. Two hundred carriages jammed the narrow streets. Schools were closed.

♠ Bach was considered a hack by the time he died, the news barely noticed. The only record of his funeral is a small note from the registry of deaths in Leipzig. It reads: "A man, age 67, Mr. Johann Sebastian Bach, musical director and singing master of St. Thomas School, was carried to his grave in the hearse, 30 July, 1750."

It's a strange world, aina'?

You don't have to wait for a full moon to realize we live in a strange world, where people say and do things that leave you wondering if you need more sleep. Some years ago I came to realize this point after a phone call from a listener. I had been talking about the Beethoven contemporary Domenico Dragonetti, a double-bass virtuoso and composer, who had such a passion for dolls that he always carried one with him and introduced it as his wife. I couldn't help laughing at my own story. The caller said he could determine from my laughter that I was having emotional problems possibly brought on by an extra marital affair. Jesus Christ, I thought to myself, scratching my head, I can't wait to tell my wife about this one. "Hey, man, don't tell my three concubines," I said to him. "They're already fighting to see who's number one."

♠ In the case of the composer Borodin, he was married to a strange woman, an insomniac, who would roam the apartment all night and keep him awake. Sometimes she would use his manuscripts to cover jars of sour milk, or to line the cat box.

♠ Luigi Piccioli, an Italian in his 60s who claimed to be in his 50s, was one of Tchaikovsky's early singing teachers. Piccioli not only had a grotesque physique, but he also painted his cheeks and dyed his hair. He wore a peculiar device in the back of his head to tighten the wrinkles in his face. To Piccioli, any music other than Italian was junk, including Beethoven and Mozart.

♠ Gertrud Wittergren, a famous soprano, insisted on being kicked three times in her *tush* before going on the stage. She said it was an old Swedish custom.

♠ Bizet studied piano with his uncle Francoise. Old Uncle Francoise had a bunch of peculiar habits, one of which he had learned from his teacher. Sometimes he would put a stack of opera books on his head, hoping that some of the musical genius would seep in.

♠ Arthur Fiedler had a particular fondness for the Number 13. He was 13th among those auditioning at the Berlin Royal Academy – and he won. His name has 13 letters. His home in Brookline, Mass., had two 13s in it.

♠ Some of Franz Liszt's admirers collected his cigar butts, while others made bracelets out of his broken piano strings.

♠ Don Juan's legend is based on the life of Don Juan Tenorio Y Salazar, the 14th-century Spanish nobleman, who had many love affairs and broke many young hearts. Finally a group of fathers lured him to a monastery and murdered him. As a cover up, they convinced the police that a stone statue had come to life and carried Don Juan to the land beyond. Mozart and scores of other composers wrote operas based on Don Juan.

When I worked at WNIB in Chicago, some guy sent me the following little number in a hand-scribbled note. I don't know where he found the material, unless he was the original source. Although the note was postmarked somewhere in North Carolina (He must have listened to the show via the Internet), it came without a name and return address. He closed his letter with "Don't you think Wagner is the source of all light?" Beats me, brother. The guy reminded me of a serial killer in hiding. The note is long gone, but I did manage to copy some of it in my notebook back then:

♠ "I know you have loads of interest in numerology," he wrote. (*I do? Since when?*) "Consider Wagner's case. Number 13 plays big in his life. Wagner was born in 1813. The elements of that number together add up to 13 – like 1 and 8, 1 and 3. There are 13 letters in Richard Wagner. He played in public first in 1831. Elements of that number add up to 13 – 1 and 8, 3 and 1. Tannhauser was finished in 1844 – on April 13. They first played the opera in Paris in 1861 – on March 13. The first time the Ring Cycle began playing was in 1876 – on August 13. He wrote 13 operas. He was exiled 13 years. Died February 13 in the 13th year of the new German Confederation." *Sure, Wagner's the source of all light if you're a serial killer in hiding.*

♠ Pierre Augustin Beaumarchais, the playwright who in 1775 created *The Barber of Seville*, was also a gunrunner, a spy, and a clockmaker. Beaumarchais married a number of rich women all of whom died a short time later.

♠ Lawrence Tibbett always stood on his head several minutes before making a public appearance.

♠ Princess Carolyn Sayn-Wittgenstein, one of the loveliest women of her day who for a time was Liszt's mistress, loved to sprawl on a bearskin rug naked. Sayn-Wittgenstein, who also smoked cigars, had a fear of fresh air. She sealed her windows, and made visitors wait in an anteroom to be properly devitalized.

♠ The six-year-old Haydn was sent to live with a cousin in Heinburg for more musical opportunities. When the church's drummer died, Haydn had to learn to play the drums in order to take over the position. Since he was small, for the Holly Week Procession, a drum was tied to the back of the local hunchback and Haydn followed behind him with his drumsticks. *Gene Krupa, eat your heart out.*

♠ Paganini, the great showman, always gave concerts wearing red and yellow clothing, with blue-tinted eyeglasses. The getup heightened his cadaverous appearance even more. If he accidentally touched some people, they would quickly cross themselves. Some also thought the G String on his violin was fashioned from his wife's intestine.

♠ Jascha Heifetz, David Oistrakh, Nathan Milstein and Isaac Stern were all great violinists and they all came from Odessa, Russia. *Maybe it was the yogurt.*

♠ An Englishman counted the measures in some of Wagner's operas and came up with these numbers: *Das Rheingold* has 3906 bars; *Parsifal* 4347 bars; and *The Flying Dutchman* 4432 bars. *Talk about somebody with nothing better to do.*

♠ Louis Antoine Julienne, a flamboyant conductor whose symphony concerts were more like lavish musicals, finally outdid himself by trying to set the Lord's Prayer to music. Although he failed to complete the piece, in a letter to a friend he wrote: "Think what a grand title: *The Lord's Prayer, words by Jesus Christ, music by Julienne.*"

♠ Georg Matthias Monn (1717-1750), a composer and organist who mostly worked in Vienna, had a weak physical constitution, was gloomy, and always wore black clothes. He refused to drink wine. *No hope for the guy.*

♠ With his mind constantly swirling with ideas, sometimes Schubert slept with his glasses on. It was so that he would save time searching for his glasses just in case he got an idea in the middle of the night.

♠ By 1744, Sylvius Leopold Weiss (1686-1958), a dominating composer of lute music, was the highest paid musician at the Dresden Court. In 1722, a French violinist named Petite bit Weiss's thumb in a fight, almost severing it at the first joint. It was a year before Weiss could play the lute again.

♠ Conductors' antics and idiosyncrasies are legend. After accusing the bassist of inattention during rehearsal, the autocratic composer and conductor Christoph Willibald Von Gluck crept up to the fellow on his knees and pinched him on the *tokhus*. The bassist yelped and he and his bass fiddle went crashing to the floor. *I have no idea what happened after that.*

♠ A team of researchers at the University of Texas once rigged loudspeakers in the cages of two groups of rats. Mozart played to one group and Schoenberg to the other. The Mozart group got along fine, whereas the Schoenberg group was agitated and quarrelsome.

♠ Dvorak was frightened of thunderstorms. When he knew of an approaching storm, he would cancel his lessons and refuse to see anyone. During the storm he would try to drown out the sound of thunder with loud chords on his piano.

♠ Johann Strauss Sr. poured beer into his violin to mellow the tone.

♠ Tchaikovsky had stage fright early on. The first time he conducted an orchestra – in music from his opera *Voyevoda* – he was so terrified, so desperate to run away and hide that he forgot some sections and gave all the wrong leads. Fortunately the players knew the piece and saved the day. Later he told a friend that in his panic he felt his head would fall off his shoulders unless he held it firmly in place, and that he kept a tight grip on his bearded chin throughout the work.

♠ Paganini was such a great violinist that people began thinking he was in cahoots with the Devil. It got to be so bad that Paganini's mother had to publish a letter in his defense, explaining that all that freaky stuff about her boy was untrue.

♠ Handel endured much frustration from his temperamental performers. During the London production of his opera *Astianatte*, two of his prima donnas got into a slugfest, right on the stage. Francesca Cuzzoni and Faustina Bordoni, Italian imports whose rivalry was so great that two racehorses were named after them, had demanded Handel write equal numbers of arias for them. Handel had done so. *What caused the fight is anybody's guess.*

♠ Until age 10 Mozart had a pathological fear of the trumpet and the French horn, when played as a solo instruments.

♠ Haydn died in the early hours of May 31, 1809, and was buried in a Vienna cemetery. In 1820, his remains were transferred to Eisenstadt, the estate just over the Hungarian border where he had been music director for Prince Nickolas Esterhazy for about 30 years. Sometime later the grave was opened and the head found missing. Story has it that two of Haydn's friends had bribed the gravediggers at the funeral to remove the head. From 1895 until 1954, the skull rested in the museum of the *Gesellschaft den Musikfreunde* in Vienna. In 1954, the head was finally placed with the rest of Haydn's body at the *Berkirche* at Eisenstadt.

♠ Antonin Dvorak, a train freak, said that he would rather have invented the locomotive than composed his symphonies. In Prague, he spent considerable time at the Franz Josef station, frequently writing down locomotive numbers. Dvorak, acquainted with almost everyone who worked at the station, knew the train timetables by heart so that when a train was late, he would argue with the officials, and sometimes apologize to passengers for the delay. On the days he was busy, he would send his students to the station to write the numbers of express trains leaving for European capitols. One day he sent his student Josef Suk, who was to become his son-in-law, and Suk returned with the numbers of coal tenders instead of engines. Dvorak shook his head and in good humor said, "To think that I am letting a man like you marry my daughter." In New York City, he was not allowed on the train platform unless a passenger and Dvorak could not enjoy the same intimate relationship with train workers. So he would take an overhead tram to 155th St. There, he would stand and watch the Chicago and Boston Express go by. Soon Dvorak turned his attention to steamships, visiting many in port and inspecting them from stern to stern. He got to know the captains and the mates by name.

♠ Pushkin wrote some of *Eugene Onegin*, his novel-in-verse, while sprawled across a friend's billiards table. Tchaikovsky used the story for his opera *Eugene Onegin*.

♠ In 1827, after his father's death in Bologna, and with Paris not all that receptive to him as an artist, Liszt slipped into such a state of depression that one Paris publication ran his obituary: "Franz Liszt, Oct. 22, 1811, died Paris, 1828." Liszt had to come out of his depression, because he had his mother to support. So he began teaching.

♠ Rossini, being naturally lazy, sometimes wore two wigs, one on top of the other, so that he wouldn't have to bother taking the bottom one off.

♠ One of the most famous portraits of Stravinsky is a line drawing by Picasso. Italian border guards once stopped Stravinsky after finding the portrait in his luggage and concluding that it was a map of Italian secret fortifications. It took Stravinsky a while to convince them otherwise. *Come on, guys, give me a break.*

♠ Even as a little boy, Tchaikovsky was obsessed with music. After a family party once, his governess Fanny Durbach found him sitting up in bed and crying, complaining that music kept playing in his head. "Oh, this music, this music," he cried, tapping his head. "Oh, this music, this music – take it away."

♠ In 1791, when Mozart was ill, tired and broke, a mysterious man appeared at his door to commission a requiem mass for the soul of a departed friend. He insisted the commission be kept a secret. "What is this?" declared Mozart. "Am I writing my own funeral music? Has my clock run out? Am I to die at 35?" About two months later, on December 4, 1791, friends came over to help him work on the mass. Later that day he gave further instructions for completion of the mass to his friend Franz Xaver Sussmayer. Sometime after midnight Mozart died. Twenty years later a man named Leutgeb, from a village in lower Austria, confessed before his death that he had been the mystery man who appeared at Mozart's door. The commission for the mass had come from a Count Von Walsegg, who apparently had the dubious habit of commissioning music, copying the score in his own handwriting and publishing it under his own name. The count's wife had died in 1791, and the requiem mass he had commissioned from Mozart was for her. The count obtained the mass from Constanza, Mozart's wife, after the composer's death and had it performed two years later as his own work. When Constanza discovered the truth, she had the mass performed in Vienna under Mozart's name. The count brought a lawsuit against Constanza, but it was settled out of court with the count losing under much humiliations.

Mind your P's and Q's

*I*t is no secret today that propriety and good manners are extinct like the watch and chain. When I was morning announcer on WNIB, Chicago, a crotchety man called me on the studio phone off the air about 6:40 a.m. one day to complain about the Bach violin concerto I was playing. "Of all the beautiful music in the world you have to play this shit," he barked. "Yes, doesn't it get the juices flowing?" I teased. He must have slammed the phone down. Another morning, a gentleman with an English accent phoned to say that although he found the Rachmaninoff I was playing pleasing, he would have preferred to hear it perhaps an hour or two later in the show. "At this hour," he added, "I like my tea with two lumps of sugar." Now, is that class or what? I figure it this way: If the pen is mightier than the sword, then the refined mouth is stronger than the one with the foot in it.

♠ Luigi Boccherini, who worked in a number of European courts, joined Charles IV, king of Spain, and Joseph II, the emperor of Austria, in their respective courts to play trios and quartets. Joseph II once asked him whether he, the emperor, played better than the Spanish king. Boccherini replied, "Sire, Charles IV plays like a *king*, but your Imperial Highness plays like an *emperor*."

♠ Emperor Francis I of Austria, an amateur violinist, once sat in as first violin for rehearsals with a string quartet. The performance was a disaster, since old Francis ignored all the *flats*. So the composer of the piece finally said, "Would your Majesty grant my humble prayer for a most gracious *B-flat*?"

189

♠ King George III of England took violin lessons from Johann Peter Salomon. After a few lessons, Salomon summed up his royal experience to the king this way: "Fiddlers, Your Majesty, may be divided into three classes. To the first belong those who cannot play at all; to the second those who play badly; and to the third those who play well. You, Sire, have already achieved the second class."

♠ A wealthy American hostess thought the Polish pianist and composer Ignacy Paderewski was a polo player. "No," Paderewski said. "He is a rich soul who plays polo. I am a poor Pole who plays solo."

♠ One night at the opera, Emperor Napoleon III asked Rossini to join him in his box. Rossini apologized for being unprepared with the proper attire. The emperor replied: "Do me the honor of sitting next to me, Maestro Rossini, and please remember that ceremony is unnecessary between emperors."

♠ Austrian Emperor Josef II dismissed Mozart after an undiplomatic remark by the composer. After hearing *Abduction from the Seraglio*, the emperor said, "My dear Mozart, it's certainly a very charming opera, but I believe it is a bit subtle for our ears. There are too many notes in the score." Mozart replied: "I beg Your Majesty's pardon, but there are just as many notes in my score as are necessary." The emperor dismissed him, saying, "I am sure you should be the best judge of that."

♠ During a performance in London, Heifetz noticed the queen smiling at him. He returned the smile and kept on playing. The next morning a messenger from Buckingham Palace informed him that the king wished to see him. Heifetz, alarmed, declared, "But, believe me, she smiled at me first."

♠ A young pianist advertised her Berlin recital claiming to have been Franz Liszt's student. She had never even seen Liszt, of course. By chance Liszt showed up in Berlin just before her concert. The pianist, panicking, confessed the deception to Liszt. Liszt graciously invited her to play the program in his apartment, and gave her some hints. Then he wished her luck, saying, "Now, my dear, you can call yourself a pupil of Liszt."

♠ "You have certainly worked hard," Archduchess Sophie said to Joseph Lanner after a long night of music. "Yes, Your Imperial Highness, I sure did," Lanner replied, wiping sweat from his face. He then took off his coat and added, "Look at how I am sweating." Just for that bit of impropriety he was promptly fired from his duty.

♠ "As for my feelings, I shall never be calculating and politic," said Schubert. "I come straight out with what is in me, and that's that."

♠ With little patience for pretentious or boring people, Schubert chose his friends not because of what he could get out of them, but because he wanted to be with them. He was interested in what people did for a living. On meeting new people, he would always ask, "*Kanner was?*" (What do you do?)

♠ "I love music more than my own convenience," said conductor George Szell. "Actually I love it more than myself, but it is vastly more loveable than I."

♠ Playing at a soiree in St. Petersburg, Liszt noticed Tsar Nicholas talking loudly to a lady. Liszt stopped abruptly and walked away. "Why have you stopped playing?" the Tsar asked. "When the emperor speaks," said Liszt, "one ought to be silent."

♠ "I wish you'd display a little more tact in choosing the music," said the orchestra manager to the conductor. "We've got the National Association of Umbrella Makers here this evening, and you've just played 'It Ain't Gonna Rain No More.'"

♠ Pianist Artur Rubinstein was having coffee in a Berlin café with the Russian composer Alexadre Scriabin. "Who's your favorite composer?" asked Scriabin. "Brahms, of course," replied Rubinstein. The outraged Scriabin slammed the table and shouted, "Why isn't your favorite composer Scriabin?"

♠ Rossini was rehearsing the orchestra when the horn player squeaked a note. "What's that?" snapped Rossini. "It is I," stuttered the horn player. "Ah, is it?" said Rossini. "Then pack your horn and go home. I'll join you later." The player was Rossini's father.

♠ With Weber in Vienna for the production of his opera *Der Freischutz*, Schubert and librettist Franz Schobert sought his help in launching their grand opera *Alfonso und Estrella*. Weber said he would help, only to change his mind after Schubert said he didn't like Weber's *Euryanthe* as much as his other opera, *Der Freischutz*.

♠ On June 16, 1842, Mendelssohn dined with Queen Victoria and Prince Albert at Buckingham Palace. That evening Victoria and the other dignitaries present had a jolly time playing music and singing. Years later Victoria was proud to say that she had studied with Mendelssohn.

♠ Serge Koussevitzky visited a dying musician at the hospital. Since the musician had nothing to lose, he took a last shot at the maestro and told him off: that Koussevitzky was a tyrant, selfish, cruel and heartless. Well, the musician didn't die after all, and lived to play under Koussevitzky for a number of years. The maestro never forgave him.

♠ Cherubini and Napoleon, before Napoleon became first consul, were attending a Cherubini opera. "My dear, Cherubini," said Napoleon, "you are certainly an excellent musician, but really, your music is so noisy and complicated that I can make nothing of it." Cherubini replied, "My dear general, you are certainly an excellent soldier, but in regard to music, you must excuse me if I don't think it necessary to adopt my compositions to your comprehension." It was the wrong thing to say, and Cherubini had to take refuge in Vienna for a time.

♠ Rossini was rehearsing the orchestra when the oboist played an F-sharp instead of an F. Rossini corrected him, adding, "In regard to the F-sharp, you needn't be concerned. We shall find some other place to put it."

♠ Queen Victoria declared Paderewski a young genius. "Oh, Your Majesty," Paderewski replied, "a genius, perhaps, but before I was a genius, I was just a drudge."

♠ A young composer asked Mozart's advice on composition. "Begin writing simple things first, songs, for example," said Mozart. "But you composed symphonies when you were only a child," said the young composer. "Ah, but I didn't go to anybody to find out how to become a composer," said Mozart.

♠ Napoleon asked the Belgian composer Andre Gretry about the difference between Mozart and Cimarosa. "Sire," said Gretry, "Cimarosa places the statue on the stage and the pedestal in the orchestra, while Mozart puts the statue in the orchestra and the pedestal on the stage."

♠ Beethoven's neighbor Frau Fischer observed the young Beethoven sitting at his bedroom window overlooking the courtyard, holding his head in his hands, and looking pensive. "What are you looking at, Ludwig?" she inquired. Beethoven didn't answer. Later when she asked why he had ignored her, Beethoven begged her forgiveness, adding, "No answer is also an answer. I was so taken up by profound and beautiful thoughts that I could not bear to be disturbed."

♠ Liszt was speaking with King Louis Philippe of France about conditions in the 1830s Paris. "Do you remember the time you played at my house as a little boy when I was yet Duke of Orleans?" asked the king. "Things have greatly changed since then." Liszt said, "Yes, Sire, but not for the better." Liszt was due to receive the Legion of Honor, but not after that insult.

♠ Mendelssohn loved England and the English, but he thought the concert audiences peculiar, since they did everything from pushing past people and overturning chairs to chattering loudly and munching on food noisily. He said some people didn't care what they heard or saw as long as it didn't interfere with their activity.

♠ After hearing Paderewski's concert, Tsar Nicholas II announced how pleased he was that a Russian should achieve such great world fame. Paderewski said he was not a Russian but a Pole – and that was the last time he was heard in concert in Russia.

♠ In London, while rehearsing the opera *Ottone*, Handel's temperamental Italian import Francesca Cuzzoni demanded Handel pack her big aria with extra high notes or else she would not sing it. Handel, refusing to put up with such insolence, held her over the edge of an open window and demanded she cooperate or down she went. (*That was one method of executing criminals in Germany.*) When she gave in, Handel declared, "Look, I know you're a witch, but don't forget I'm the devil himself."

♠ Rossini, in London as guest of King George IV, asked the king to sing and that he would accompany him at the piano. The king made one mistake after another, which Rossini ignored. Later the king congratulated him on his tact. Rossini replied diplomatically, "Sire, it is my duty to accompany you – even to hell."

THE END

Index

200